Volume 2 | Fylde Coast, Lake District and Cumbria

Illustrations (cover and inside): William Eagar
@william.eagar.golf

Published by 18Players.com

ISBN 978-1-9162106-6-0

linksfromtheroad.com

Welcome

Volume 2 takes me gently away from my home patch and into Cumbria. It's the beginning of the journey proper and I am thrilled to have you along for company

THANK you so much to everyone who supported Volume 1 of this series. Sharing the stories and memories of these courses truly is a privilege, but the number of messages of support received from readers around the world was enormously gratifying. Thank you.

I'm hopeful the series can develop as we travel clockwise around the country. In Volume 1, it was the courses close to home I was writing about. In some ways, the places most familiar are harder to write about. The courses featuring in Volume 2 are still only a short day out from my home on the Wirral Peninsula, but there were plenty I encountered for the first time during the tour. Again, I'm hoping there'll be a good mix of courses well known to all, some you may have heard of and a few complete unknowns. Over time, I'm hoping this series will grow into a collection for those who love links golf. A reference series for planning future trips to experience the courses for yourself.

I am sure many of you know that my 'day job' is as a golf course architect. Formerly the British Architectural Associate for the firm of Clayton, DeVries & Pont, I'm now a partner in a new firm: McDonnell & Cooper. Joe McDonnell, my colleague at CDP and longtime friend beforehand, is an extraordinary talent. He brings enormous technical skills to the partnership, allowing us to showcase our designs as well as anyone in the world. Of the courses you read about in Volume 1, we are proud to now work with both Formby and Hesketh. Our young firm has attracted clients from across Britain already, and we hope to continue to grow.

Based on some of the generous feedback to Volume 1, I have taken a slightly deeper look at the courses featured in Volume 2. Perhaps I was originally worried this series would only attract readers if I kept it 'mainstream'. But I think those concerns were misplaced. Two suggestions in particular encouraged me to embrace the architectural perspective.

The first came from Dan Davies, a writer I've long admired. Dan is an award-winning author. He also happens to be the proprietor of 'RNGC', a nine-hole backyard course set on one acre of former orchard at his beautiful family home in Devon. He encouraged me to give in to the architectural analysis temptation.

Another Dan, this time my ever-patient editor Dan Murphy, suggested the Favourite Holes section of Volume 1 could be expanded into a longer Eclectic 18 section. This is where I've taken the words 'deep dive' and 'longer' a little too literally – but I hope you

"I've taken a slightly deeper look at the courses featured. Perhaps I was originally worried this series would only attract readers if I kept it 'mainstream'. But I think those concerns were misplaced"

enjoy this profile on some of the many compelling holes encountered along this section of coastline.

I must also give thanks to Will Eagar, who has provided the most beautiful illustrations. Will is such a talented artist, and I'm very fortunate this series can be elevated by his artwork. The cover to this book captures an imagined view of Blackpool. Those who are familiar with the area might recognise the world-famous tower or perhaps the pier. I'm sure the eagle-eyed will spot the plane landing at the airfield adjacent to St Annes Old Links.

This is a varied stretch of coastline full of high-quality courses, many of them completely overlooked. Royal Lytham & St Annes is, by some way, the best known. But the story of this club's birth, and the role St Annes Old Links plays, is one I found fascinating. Further north, Seascale and Silloth-on-Solway – both juxtaposing glorious linksland against backdrops of heavy industry – are courses worth the short detour from the M6 motorway for those journeying between England and Scotland. And in between are courses of rich history, real quirk and fabulous holes. I have no doubt it will be something I say at the beginning of each and every volume, but it was a privilege to spend time in this beautiful part of the country and play courses I'd never even heard of before.

I must thank everyone who has worked so hard on making this series a reality. There is an enormous amount of work that goes into it. If there have been teething problems while we get into our stride, I hope they weren't too painful, but between Dan, Tom, Mike, Andy, Georgina and Matthew I'm incredibly grateful for making this series a reality.

Most importantly, thanks go to my wife – Harriet. Not a golfer, she travelled the entire country with me as part of this tour. Even more, she has read every word of this series multiple times. I'm so very fortunate to have a wife who not only lets me indulge my love of links golf and course architecture but supports me wholeheartedly in doing so.

Finally, I must thank you, the reader. Without reading, buying, gifting and supporting this project in so many ways I would have the memories of an extraordinary experience – but nothing else to show for it. I hope we can continue to tell the story of each and every course I was fortunate enough to play on my two-year odyssey around Great Britain's coastline – but it is only thanks to you that I can do so.

With my thanks,

Sam

The Links and the Lakes

Welcome to a region that offers golfing surprises around every jagged corner of its varied coastline

THE great privilege of my tour was visiting regions of the Great British coastline that are often overlooked for golf. This will become more evident as the series takes us off the beaten track to islands and isolated stretches of golf that rarely feature in the golfing press.

Volume 1 did not fit this bill. A few lesser-known courses maybe, but the region dubbed as 'England's Golf Coast' is famous. With the spotlight of the 151st Open Championship directed firmly at course 001, Hoylake, this region is one of the best known we will cover in the series.

Volume 2 is the first time we venture through some unchartered golfing ground. True, the courses around the Victorian seaside resorts of Lytham and St Annes do not fit this bill, but those further north certainly do.

There are two main regions of England's far north-west coastline discussed here, as well as a detour across the Irish Sea.

This is where we find the first course of Volume 2. Castletown, as 013/225 describes, is a short hop in a propeller plane to an island not officially part of the United Kingdom.

The Isle of Man, like the isles of Jersey and Guernsey that will also feature in due course, is a Crown Dependency. Self-governing but under the protection of the United Kingdom, it is the first course we encounter away from the British mainland. There are other courses on this small island, but I am satisfied Castletown is the only one with a reasonable claim of being a links.

We then return to the mainland for courses 013 to 017, all based on the Fylde Coast. This is a region famed for its golf, home to Royal Lytham & St Annes and an extraordinary history. With the equally famous Victorian seaside town of Blackpool to the north, it was a region that exploded in popularity and expansion in the same era the game of golf itself was experiencing a transformative golfing boom of its own.

The River Ribble separates these courses from the Cumbrian stretch to the north. Cumbria – wild, rugged and remote – is the last English county we will explore before crossing the Scottish border in Volume 3. Home to contrasting landscapes, it is bookended by beautiful courses juxtaposed against industrial backdrops – namely Furness to the south and Silloth to the north.

In between lie the mountains, fells, rivers and lakes of the Lake District National Park. A region of jaw-dropping beauty, William Wordsworth once described it as 'the loveliest spot that man hath found'. But while millions of holidaymakers seek out the soaring tranquillity of the Lakes each year, few golfers visit the coastline in their morning shadow. Highlights of the region are plenty – but please do not make the mistake of the majority and skip past Castletown, Seascale or Silloth in this volume.

Royal Lytham is another favourite, but not one that could claim a lack of awareness. However, St Annes Old Links, the course that played a key role in the birth of its famous neighbour, is often overlooked.

Unlike Volume 1, there is no single place to stay

"A region of jaw-dropping beauty, Wordsworth described it as 'the loveliest spot that man hath found'. While millions of holidaymakers seek out the soaring tranquillity of the Lakes, few golfers visit the coastline in their morning shadow"

that gives you a central base to tackle each of the dozen courses featured here. The geography of the area makes it a little too complicated. But that shouldn't give you an excuse to simply drive on by. Below are some of the more interesting places to eat, drink and stay that I've either enjoyed myself or had recommended to me. If you do make the trip here, please do tell me what you think. I'd love to hear your thoughts on the places and courses featured in these pages. LFTR

The hues and shades of the Lake District present a marked contrast to the links courses that lie on its western perimeter

The Links & The Lakes

12

Courses we feature in Volume 2 of Links from the Road

09

The number of courses in this volume that have 18 holes

10

The number of holes at Dunnerholme – a one-off on the tour

01

Courses in this volume not technically in the United Kingdom – Castletown is on the Isle of Man, which is a Crown Dependency

80

Miles that separate Furness, in the south of Cumbria, and Silloth, in the north, most of them on the coastal A595

1861

The year Fleetwood Golf Club was formed – giving it a claim to be the oldest in England

168

The number of bunkers at Royal Lytham & St Annes

013/225

Castletown Golf Links

Shaped by a blessed combination of Old Tom Morris, Alister MacKenzie and Philip Mackenzie Ross, this is surely one of the most spectacular layouts the British Isles coastline has to offer

At the par-4 6th, the uneven fairway charmingly traverses a diagonal path before reaching a green that is well protected by bunkering and the natural contours

WHAT is the UK's most convenient links course to play? What a ridiculous question. Of course, it's subjective. It depends where you live, where you plan to visit. How long are you willing to travel for to play the course? There are a hundred variables and quite clearly no right answer. Well, I have a rogue suggestion. Please bear with me.

I opted to fly rather than take the ferry over to Castletown. I left my home in Hoylake just before 7am. Forty minutes later, just managing to avoid the real morning rush, I was dropping my clubs off with the smiling Logan Air attendant at Liverpool Airport. I whizzed through security and, with no immigration to worry about for a domestic flight, had the chance to enjoy a coffee in the lounge before boarding the plane. The propellers on the little aircraft, adorned in a tartan design only Scotland's national carrier could pull off, started spinning at 8.15.

Thirty minutes later, we'd landed. The conveyor belt carrying my clubs (thankfully – it's always a relief seeing them) was just jolting into action as we walked into the terminal at Ronaldsway Airport and the dozen of us on the flight wandered out to the waiting line of taxis.

Out the expectant driver jumped, loading the clubs into the boot and asking how the journey had been. We had barely asked about his island home before we pulled into the car park of Castletown Golf Links eight minutes later. I checked my watch: 9.05.

From door to 1st tee, with no stress and little effort, it had barely taken two hours.

It made me think how many others lived within an hour's drive of the nine domestic airports that directly link with Ronaldsway: Three in London, Bristol, Birmingham, Manchester, Liverpool, Glasgow and Edinburgh. With the help of my old calculator and some rather dry government data, I worked out that there are over 44 million people living in such proximity. That's 44 million people, 62 per cent of the country, who are maybe two-and-a-half hours from the 1st tee of Castletown. All of them able to play a round in the morning, a second in the afternoon and still go to sleep in their own bed that same night.

But is it worth the trip? Well, how many links courses can you think of that are able to thank Old Tom Morris, Alister MacKenzie and Philip MacKenzie-Ross (associate of the great Tom Simpson, the man who gave us Southerness and Turnberry) for their design? How many can you think of that see the ocean from every single hole? How many are flanked by water on three sides of the course? How many demand heroic drives and mid irons struck with conviction over crashing waves and gnarled rocks? There aren't many, and too many golfers are missing out on something special.

Being a crown dependency of the UK, rather than an official part of the country, the Isle of Man sets

many of its own laws. As a result, the island is well known as a tax haven and for having no speed limit. This gives way to another famous export, the Isle of Man TT. Almost every year since 1907, 37.73 miles of the island's roads become a racetrack for the world's most daring motorcyclists.

The top speed recorded during the race was set in 2023 at 206mph, and the average speed across the whole route has exceeded 136mph.
But golf made the trip to the island some years before the motorcycles started racing. In 1891, it was a man of enormous power and influence in Douglas who had encouraged Old Tom Morris to make the journey.

A view of the T-shaped peninsula that Castletown occupies, offering sea views on each and every hole

Alexander Bruce was a Scot who had himself been coaxed to the island by a wealthy entrepreneur, George William Dumbell. Dumbell had a wide range of business interests, but prize among them was the bank run under his own name. Bruce was brought in to run Dumbells Bank in 1878 and grew it to the point it served almost all on the island.

In 1891, Bruce organised and paid for Old Tom's visit – with the assured knowledge that golf was an import the entire island would benefit from. In addition to Castletown, Old Tom laid out two other

courses – one parkland and one clifftop. Ramsey Golf Club, the parkland course, has been expanded from the 12-hole course Old Tom laid out – and the trees absent from the early photographs of the course have naturally grown beyond recognition. Port-e-Chee Links has been renamed as King Edward's Bay Golf Club and is a classic clifftop layout.

The club at Castletown came after Old Tom's visit, founded in 1892. Over 130 years later, I found myself thanking the foresight of Mr Bruce – but unfortunately his legacy is not so appreciated on the island. In 1900, there was a run on Dumbells Bank which led to its collapse. The result was catastrophic for the economy of the island – and the directors of the bank were arrested for fraud. The man who had been dubbed the 'Uncrowned King of the Isle of Man' found his reputation in tatters. He died before the trial, a few months after his arrest. His funeral was attended only by his closest relatives, while an article at the time observed "had he died a year earlier, half of Douglas would have followed his coffin".

The course at Castletown, though, went from strength to strength. By 1913, it was the turn of the good Doctor, Alister MacKenzie, to make significant contributions to the layout. Unfortunately, the precise details of what changes were made are unknown – but praise for the course in its new guise was lavish.

After the Second World War, Philip Mackenzie-Ross made his contribution. Mackenzie-Ross might be the least known of these greats, but he is a favourite of mine. For many years, Mackenzie-Ross was an associate of the great Tom Simpson. To put it mildly, Simpson suffered no fools. Simply to hold the position speaks to his intellect and perspicacity. After the war, Mackenzie-Ross was the man commissioned to rebuild the famed Ailsa course at Turnberry. He laid out a new course at Southerness and made some significant changes to Castletown. A feature of his style evident at all three of these courses is the dramatic use of the coast. Turnberry is, of course, most famous for this meeting of land and sea – but Southerness and its glorious 12th hole provides another example.

Castletown could be the best of the lot. The course is laid out in a 'T' shape – navigating the peninsula of land it occupies. The first few holes are very much 'internal', nice enough, with interesting bunkering and some particularly satisfying green complexes. The 4th is the start of a great little run, a dogleg left around a sheer drop to the adjacent fairway below.

The 5th is one of the most photographed holes on the course. This doglegs right, sweeping in cape style around a bay and the club's entrance road. Both holes have such wonderful bones but are truly let down by the amount of gorse that has been allowed to grow on the face of the hill that separates them. The 4th would be a wonderful risk/reward hole if some of the corner could be cut off on the drive or approach, but the volume of gorse there just removes all desire to take on an exhilarating shot.

On the 5th, the gorse punishes those who are worried about making the carry and instead bail left. From this side, the hole is made far longer and the bunkering for the approach makes it an incredibly difficult approach anyway. I would imagine the local members opt for an iron off the tee on both occasions, more concerned with keeping their ball than anything else.

The 6th might feature as one of the more underrated holes on the links. The one thing the course does not boast in spades is holes of characterful rumpled links fairways. This is certainly one of them, and the road cutting diagonally across this fairway is the kind of quirky feature the old architects would have loved. The next is a long par 5, culminating in one of the most interesting greens on the course, offering three tiers of torment, before we arrive on one of the most extraordinary par 3 tees you'll find anywhere. There are no bunkers on the 8th hole, but that is exactly the

Judicious gorse clearance could make the par-4 4th and 5th holes even more exciting by increasing the risk-and-reward element

The closing hole hugs the coastline and demands an approach over the rocks to find the elusive two-tiered green beyond

required number. It's the far point of the property and the moment at which we turn back towards the main bulk of land. To the right, Castletown Bay laps almost to the tee. The hole, like many of the others here, is rather overgrown. Managed properly and with the beautiful shapes under the vegetation exposed – it could be a special hole indeed.

No 9 is another potential classic. A split height fairway – the right half along the bay is just wide enough for an accurate driver to try and find. Most will end up safely down the left, approaching a green over a string of bunkers, pitched away from them and with the putting surface just high enough to repel anything other than the perfect approach. The benefit of taking on the risk of the drive is immediately apparent once you've stood on the green and looked back down this marvellous hole.

The 10th is another beauty. From a tee back on the water's edge – the risk of the bay will naturally force the majority left – only leading to another approach. Holding your nerve and line is a skill the members of Castletown must have honed through the years.

The run from 11 to 15 is nice golf – but not of the order we've now become accustomed to. This is

former agricultural land that feels as if it was brought into the design later. But before we accept the heady heights we enjoyed earlier in the round have passed, we reach the 16th tee. When I suggested earlier that Castletown might encapsulate Mackenzie-Ross's love of marrying golf and the sea better even than Turnberry, this closing stretch is what I had in mind. We have gradually climbed from the low point by the 8th tee to stand astride rocky cliffs with the Irish Sea crashing and swirling far below.

With such a dramatic backdrop, the architect used remarkable restraint to build a green that sits comfortably within it, but without trying to take centre stage. A single bunker sits on the fore side, the green stretched around the back edge of it. Any ball moving right to left on the wind will struggle to find the putting surface. It's a shot for the player who can master their ball flight in the full teeth of the wind.

If 16 was the warm-up of this stretch, 17 must be the main event. I struggle to think of another hole, across the entire tour, quite as dramatic as this. There are a range of tee boxes available, but the most dramatic is located halfway along a rocky promontory – necessitating a drive fully over those crashing waves and waiting rocks. The fairway seemingly requires a carry beyond the wit of all but the longest hitters, but is not quite as far as the scale and drama of the setting make it seem. LFTR

IN my day-to-day life, I spend more time looking at black and white photographs of golf courses than is probably healthy. I think even the most determined modernist might grudgingly glance at an old aerial hanging in a far corner of a spike bar and wonder how far removed it is from the course they know intimately well.

We do this not just because we're complete nerds – although that does help – but because we can learn so much from it. Churchill, as ever, said it best. The farther back you can look, the farther forward you are likely to see. Every single course laid out by one of the greats, be it Colt, MacKenzie, Braid or Morris, is rightly proud of their architectural provenance. They might print it on the scorecard or emblazon it on the website. They might create alliances or play matches against other courses with the same architect. In some way, big or small, they will care.

The reason great names are worth mentioning, even a century later, is self-evident. They created bodies of work that have stood the test of time. Courses that are enjoyed and played to this day. They refined their ideas and philosophies over their lives and careers and laid down the physical embodiments of them for us to enjoy.

A view of Fairhaven's 9th hole, which travels back to the clubhouse before setting forth again around this spacious site

014/225

Fairhaven

James Braid and Jack Steer created an unusual and highly imaginative inland links close to Lytham. Its treasures are still there, just waiting to be uncovered once more.

However, unlike many other art forms, a golf course cannot be fixed in time. But grass will grow, trees will self-seed and changes in golfing culture, technology and expectations will all mean the courses must evolve too.

With good management, and perhaps the assistance of an architect comfortable in leaving their ego at the door, we have seen how it is possible to keep a course relevant to the game of today while maintaining the design ideals, strategies and individual fingerprint of the original designer.

And, like any true fingerprint, those made on Fairhaven of old must be unique. I have not seen anywhere else in Britain that had such a distinct and recognisable course as the one James Braid laid out, with the assistance of Jack Steer, back in 1924.

This wasn't Fairhaven's first course. There was a 12-hole course built in 1892, a few years before the club itself was founded in 1895. Sandwiched between a growing school and a tidal lake, the club opted to move to flat (but sandy) land within the grounds of Lytham Hall.

With a blank canvas to work from, Braid and Steer set about their alchemy. The routing takes the

Muirfield approach of an outer and inner pair of 9s, the 9th green returning to the clubhouse. With the varied routing making full use of the spacious property, the pair turned their attention to creating the playing interest. To do so, they created some of the most bold and interesting series of ridges and swales along almost every hole. While they might have been accused of being somewhat penal, no one could suggest they lacked ambition, individuality, and character in abundance.

They created a course worthy of the 'inland links' title. The fairways were said to be fast and running, built on the sandy, free draining ground. The broken, sand-filled ground flanking the fairways must have offered a pastiche of the sand dunes of the true links. I would imagine to the refined palates of the distinguished golfers of the Roaring Twenties, this was the height of modernity. A links course without the funny bounces, perhaps even the evolution of the style.

Over the years, Fairhaven has become a course that is mainly treelined and has gained a more parkland feel

I was therefore particularly excited to explore this bold and distinctive inland links I had admired in the photographs. Unfortunately, little remains.

Close to the sea, Fairhaven is built on some excellent soil and has many holes that are infused with character

The routing is still very good, and the course itself is very enjoyable. Fairhaven is a thriving members' club, one of the busiest in the region. I have no doubt the course there is exactly as the club's members wish it to be, but I can't pretend I wasn't a little sad to see a normal golf course covering up the unique one it had once been.

There are 118 bunkers across the course, most the product of an overhaul in the 1970s and tinkering thereafter. The clear landscape that Bernard Darwin described, devoid of trees, is also lost. It is now a course where the definition is provided by scrub woodland, rhododendrons and leggy gorse.

The firm turf returns during the hot summer months, I am sure, but is unfortunately absent for the rest of the year. With the trees reducing the airflow, casting shade, and dropping leaf litter each year to add rich nutrients into the ground as they decompose, it is little wonder this facet has long since been lost. I am told the sand is still there, just beneath the surface, but I'm not sure you could tell.

I hope the reader will not misunderstand the above. I understand that courses change, that requirements for them move on. Furthermore, I understand that the maintenance involved in presenting those wide fairways with their sandy extremities might have proved prohibitively expensive for the club. Fairhaven remains an excellent course, with good greens and some interesting holes.

But if I was offered a ride in a time machine to play Braid and Steer's bold creation as it was intended, I would gladly accept. LFTR

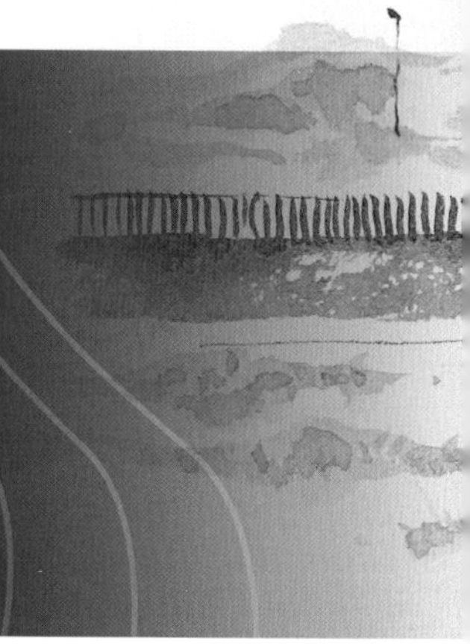

Architectural musings: The Fylde Threes

A CURIOSITY I observed on the tour at large was how the same feature or type of hole can be found repeated on courses within a certain region. There are many logical explanations for this, and still today in my professional life the underpinning forces can be felt. First among them is familiarity. Green committee members are often (not always!) more worried about avoiding a bad outcome than finding a great one. The risk of unpopular change attributed to an overzealous greens chairman carries too great a personal risk. Naturally, clubs will often look to their near neighbours and look to emulate their successes rather than disregard their peers and strike off in search of novelty.

Another reason for the phenomenon might be more powerful still. Clubs of a certain age, and within a certain region, would often have an individual person of significance in common. In the case of the Fylde Coast courses featured in this volume, George Lowe is an obvious example. At both Royal Lytham and St Annes Old Links, he was the first architect, professional and greenkeeper. Jack Steer, once an assistant professional at Lytham, helped James Braid with his 1924 work at Fairhaven, before laying out Fleetwood's 'new' course in 1932. These courses are encapsulated within the 12 miles which separate Lytham in the south to Fleetwood in the north. Therefore, in cases such as these, perhaps it is little wonder commonalities can often be observed.

In Angus (Volume 10), the use of 'burns' within the design of the links might be an example of a shared feature. Of course, it is not a feature unique to the area, but rarely do they come into play as frequently. Or, as Jean Van De Velde might attest, so consequentially. At Arbroath, the least known of these courses, 10 holes are influenced by the crossing of the Penston or Dowrie Burn. A few miles down the coast, the Buddon Burn meanders across holes at both Panmure and Monifieth, the latter a former client during my time at CDP.

With the exception of the Swilken Burn, perhaps the best-known burn in Scotland is the Barry Burn. It meanders for over 2,000 yards across Carnoustie's Championship and Burnside course – culminating in a finish where it must be crossed (at least!) five times on the closing two holes.

In Norfolk (Volume 14), the feature that immediately comes to mind is the railway-sleeper-clad bunker. Again, there are plenty of other examples from elsewhere – perhaps the famous Cape Bunker on the 4th hole at Royal North Devon the best example – but not with such ubiquity. At Great Yarmouth & Caister, the oldest course in the region, this quirky links generally played within the confines of a horseracing track (with real shades of Musselburgh) has some beautiful examples of the style. Thirty miles to the south at Aldeburgh, walls of timber line expansive swathes of sand too.

Unfortunately, Hunstanton has few remaining examples – health and safety touted as the reason for their demise. Most recent to disappear was the gorgeous cladding to the bunker short of the par-3 7th. But somewhere we can trust to resist such

The 16th at St Annes Old Links has a slightly upturned green surrounded by a menacing necklace of bunkers

modern concerns is one of my true favourite courses – Royal West Norfolk, better known as Brancaster.

Brancaster isn't the oldest club in the region, both Great Yarmouth & Caister and Hunstanton predate it, but it is surely the most significant. Timber is employed across the links both in and out of their bunkers. It is a course subject to tidal changes – the entire challenge of the course changing between high and low tide. So, the timber walls often have a practical 'retaining' role to play as well – and they achieve these practical requirements with class, character and beauty. It also brings me full circle to the forces that allow hallmarks to be shared within an area, and a prominent figure often being responsible. Brancaster's designer was no less than Horace Hutchinson. A true polymath in the Victorian era of expansion, Hutchinson was twice Amateur Champion, a prolific author and columnist on the game and captain of many of the esteemed clubs across Britain. He also grew up playing the game at Royal North Devon, home to that extraordinary Cape Bunker among other timber clad examples.

So why have I veered so tangentially away from the area in question? Rather than there being a particular shared feature in the region, I noted a hole type which cropped up time and again. It isn't so remarkable. A par 3 with a long green, pushed slightly proud of the land around it. Not by much, less than a metre for the most part. The putting surface is about 35 yards from front to back. It's narrower at the front, maybe 14 yards in width at the front third, 21 yards at the back third. From the main tee it's 160 yards to the centre of the green. Its most distinctive feature is the bunkering. A necklace of seven pots worn like an elegant choker of pearls.

Maybe an oversimplification, but this hole description suits not just the famed 9th at Lytham. It also accurately describes the 16th at St Annes Old Links. If you change the number of pot bunkers from seven to eight, it could be applied to the 17th at Fairhaven. If you dropped it down to five, so too the 8th hole at Fleetwood. What's more, if we find some old black-and-white aerials of these four holes, we see the similarities would have been even more stark than they are today. In a 1952 aerial of Lytham's 9th, 10 bunkers of a more rugged style surround the green – enhancing the V-shape of the green's tapering shape. Likewise, a 1945 aerial show 10 bunkers surrounding St Annes' 16th. There were 10 around Fairhaven's 17th in 1950 and 10 around Fleetwood's 8th in 1932. CB Macdonald, the great American architect, was famed for his 'template holes'. Versions of his 'Redan', 'Road' and 'Alps' holes can be found throughout his work.

Rather than 'cookie cutter' recreations of the exact same holes, Macdonald's templates might be better described as distinct relatives of one another. I'd go so far as to say that the 'Fylde Threes' must have been separated at birth. I resisted the urge to include any of the 'Fylde Threes' into my Eclectic 18 for the region. Any of them could have featured. LFTR

vol 2

Eclectic 18

IN Volume 1, I simply selected some of my favourite holes from the dozen courses featured between Hoylake and Hesketh. In Volume 2, I thought I should create an 'Eclectic 18' instead. The idea was to pick at least one hole from each, but no more than two from any. If a second hole was used, it had to be on the opposite nine to the first one.

The holes had to be the same number on my eclectic scorecard as they are in real life – with a nine- (or 10!) hole course providing a little wiggle room depending on if said hole was featured on the first or second loop. Finally, the course must resemble a 'genuine' one. It should be a reasonable mix of holes, reasonable par and reasonable yardage.

1st Fairhaven

523 yards, par 5

Fairhaven starts well. With the grand clubhouse immediately behind the teeing ground, it's an impressive opening. I'm always partial to a round which starts with a par 5. An opportunity to get players out and into their rounds. A bit of scoring breathing room for the majority of players, but a test of how well you can start for the better players. Especially on a course where birdie opportunities must be taken. While Fairhaven's opening hole is a good one today, it must have been brilliant in its day. The old black-and-white photographs included in this volume on the Fairhaven piece show the unique flanking expanse of sand. These extraordinary shapes, contrived during construction, are still visible today. Unfortunately, they are now full of long grass rather than sand.

2nd Maryport

428 yards, par 4

I had the luxury of selecting any of Maryport's three opening holes for this exercise. While the majority of the holes here venture inland and into the richer soils and tree-lined corridors, the opening stretch is right along Allonby Bay – on the mouth of the Solway Firth. Scotland is visible across the water. On a clear day, the lighthouse at Southerness might be a recognisable landmark. Or perhaps the inlets at Almorness Point. The tee is cut tight to the beach, which flanks the hole's left side. With the wind invariably whipping off the sea, two well-judged shots are required to thread the pair of bunkers guarding the green.

3rd Seascale
401 yards, par 4

A great hole. Seascale's 3rd lacks the beautiful setting of Maryport's 2nd. In fact, we have swapped the long sea views for a backdrop of Sellafield Nuclear Power plant. Now in the process of being decommissioned, over 1,000 buildings still sprawl over its 650-acre site. The elevated 3rd tee is the first real view of the industrial eyesore, but the golfing connoisseur will be more than capable of admiring the hole in the foreground. In many respects, it is a sister hole to the famous opener at Royal Liverpool, Hoylake. Those who are only familiar with that course (001 of this series) from the Open Championship, will recall it plays as the 3rd. Both holes play as a sharp dogleg right. At Hoylake, it is around the club's practice field. At Seascale, it is around neighbouring farmland. A small turf 'cop', only three or so feet high, offers the demarcation between fates at Hoylake. Seascale has the same, albeit topped with a barbed wire fence. Presumably, this is to keep the sheep 'in' the field, rather than any golfer looking to retrieve a Pro V1 'out'. Playing around this sharp right-angle, both holes have a fairway and green running along the very edge of the out of bounds. At Hoylake, a small and subtle hollow sits front left of the green. At Seascale, three bunkers sit along the same axis.

4th Silloth-on-Solway
370 yards, par 4

If the golfing foreground of Silloth was drawn by Harry Rowntree, the industrial backdrop might have been the work of LS Lowry. The 4th is called The Mill, the top of the eponymous structure visible above the dunes and gorse. It offers a similar visual juxtaposition to Seascale's 3rd but a different kind of golfing challenge. Rather than hold your nerve against a binary boundary hazard, this hole is all about an exacting approach to a remarkable green. The putting surface is long and narrow. No bunkers are required – instead deep and almost sheer edges give the impression you are pitching on to a tightrope. The green is 45-yards long, but across it measures 16. Many will innately understand how this style of green demands a precise approach shot but overlook the fact it requires just as accurate a drive. With firm links greens so often kicking a shot forward, playing the approach straight down the length of the green is key. A loose drive into wispy rough won't dictate an immediate punishment but will reduce distance control from an unpredictable lie and reduce the spin on landing as you play across, rather than down, this exacting green. These added layers of complexity mean the risk of missing the green, and then pitching to and fro, is real.

5th Fleetwood
441 yards, par 4

In the piece on Fleetwood, I discussed how the course has moved a number of times over a surprisingly long history. Its modern site is sheltered from the sea by a large concrete sea wall. While we might romanticise what might have been if the turf and beach melted into one another without such a stark construction, the wall clearly serves an important purpose. Without it, Fleetwood almost certainly would be lost – in part or wholly – to the sea. This question of erosion and how to protect links landscape is one which will feature significantly in later volumes of this series – particularly by the time we reach the east coast. In the meantime, we must content ourselves with imagining the proximity of sand and waves. They are just on the other side of the barrier, with the run of holes from the 3rd to the 7th running along the seaward side of Fleetwood's protected boundary. The 3rd and 6th are two strong par-3s, both of which could merit inclusion. But I opted for the 5th as a real test of ball striking. Another long par-4, it bares its teeth without becoming a bully. The undulations confirm its links authenticity, and the urban vistas which dominate the early holes of the round are replaced with an expansive view across a true coastal scene.

6th Castletown

385 yards, par 4

Castletown remains one of the most interesting sites for golf I've ever seen. It's something like a letter T, the tail connecting it to the Isle of Man at large.
It affords varied views across different bodies of water. The closing stretch of holes runs across the top of the T – 70 miles of open water between the golf course and the English coast. By contrast, either side of the T's leg are sandy coves. Here, the land is less craggy and more of a traditional links character. This hole marks a transition to the true links holes around the turn – culminating in the stretch of 8 to 11 wrapped around the spectacular Castletown Bay. Most will remember this section particularly fondly, but I thought this 6th hole was worth a mention. Rather than being a simple conduit from one point of interest to the next, it elegantly incorporates both of these wonderful vistas while still presenting an intriguing hole.

A sliced drive off the 6th tee might well carry the club's entrance road and find the beach. Assuming the ignominy of searching for an errant drive among the dog walkers on Derbyhaven Beach has been avoided, the approach towards Castletown Bay is glorious.

An access road to nearby farmland cuts diagonally across the fairway. With the great strategic architect Philip Mackenzie-Ross having consulted here, I am sure it is no coincidence it sits at such a vexing angle. If a drive has been struck long and true, this single-track road might escape your notice entirely. However, miss the fairway and look to lay up, or perhaps seek to run a ball down the rolling ground and into the well bunkered green, and there's every chance the road sits exactly where you'd want to pitch your ball. On a golf course which has no shortage of outlandish drama, I thought the 6th was an exercise of routing intelligence and disciplined restraint worthy of quiet recognition.

7th Dunnerholme

262 yards, par 4

There are only 10 holes at Dunnerholme, the only course I played with this distinction. There are plenty of nine-hole courses, and there's even a 12-holer (a great one at that).

I've included two holes from Dunnerholme in this list, and the 7th is not technically the first of them you'd come across if playing the course conventionally. I will explain why later in this list.

Health and safety has probably had a logical (if detrimental) effect on Dunnerholme's 7th. Historically, the drive was a thing of pure adrenaline. From a tee on the edge of Dunnerholme Rock, the curious flat-topped hill which gives the course its name, the fairway appears as a distant landing strip.

Between the two points, the tops of some trees sit beyond the Rock's edge – as well as the slate roofs of a couple of cottages. It's not a long carry, but even the 100 yards to carry the residents' parked cars might justify the new forward tee.

The rest of the hole is simplicity itself. A green free of any bunkers, but with the small matter of a stone wall running directly across the face of it. Unlike 'The Pit' at North Berwick, I can't pretend it offers the same strategic quandary about how exactly a drive might be positioned relative to its angle. But it is fun as hell.

All of this with 360-degree panoramic views from the tee. Not to mention a hole playing towards the hills of the southern Lake District. Some might view the course having only 10 holes as a negative. I say it's an opportunity to enjoy it twice.

8th Royal Lytham & St Annes
416 yards, par 4

Like many of Lytham's holes, it is the green and the bunkering which creates the challenge. In this case, it's how both work with the railway line – a feature down the right side of a number of front-nine holes. The fairway is pretty sedate here. Far fewer fairway pots line this hole than other holes on the famed links – but it's far from a straightforward driving hole.

The most obvious bunkering quirk employed on this hole are the three yawning cross bunkers some 60 yards short of the green's centre. With the flat fairway running hard into this militaristic abutment, the visual effect foreshortens the approach shot significantly.

It's a trick of scale and relativity which always confounds. Nowadays, there will scarcely be a single golfer to approach the green without full knowledge of the yardage. But even then, bringing yourself to trust the club in your hand when your eyes tell you it simply must be too much, is powerful.

Next is the significance of the left greenside bunker. Not only is the green angled towards the railway line, but it is almost wrapped around this left side pot. Like the Road Hole bunker on St Andrew's 17th – it also possesses a gravitational pull far greater than it warrants.

It means a drive down the right side of the fairway – one brave enough to stand up to the finality of the railway line – is justly rewarded.

Obscured by the cross bunkers, it is a test of drive and approach. The kind of exacting precision which Lytham has forged a reputation on.

9th St Annes Old Links
173 yards, par 3

This hole really is special. St Annes doesn't have particularly grand duneland. There is a particularly boisterous section by the grand clubhouse – but the majority of the holes play across more subtle terrain. After holes winding in almost every direction, tacking this way and that against the ever-present wind, the 9th plays into the heart of the dunes.

The green is long – almost 50 yards from front to back. But what it gives in depth, it takes in width. Its broadest section is only 13 yards, but a more representative width might be more like 11.

There are plenty of reasons to remember this hole. Obviously, its novelty factor is certainly one of them. The way it sits at the base of a rugged fissure, the tall nautical flagpole offering a fluttering visualisation of which way the wind plans on steering your ball. The bunkers, cut as they are at different heights and levels through the natural amphitheatre, set against the Victorian clubhouse. But the reason I particularly like the hole is for the questions it asks. Very few par-3s will tempt good players into changing their strategy from one day to the next. Even fewer will offer a range of options in the moment. The 11th hole at St Andrews is one example. The enormous green with pockets and plateaus asks whether you plan on being bold or conservative from the tee. Another is Troon's wonderful Postage Stamp. The long green there is wider at the front, tapering away past the Coffin Bunker.

Even subconsciously, the very act of getting pin high can be a decision in ambition. To a front flag, the shot might be under 140 yards. To the back? It could be 180. Depending on the firmness of the green, plus the wind, there might be as many as four clubs between a short putt and a monster. And with it? Increasing demands on accuracy, directly in line with increased complexity.

It might appear innocuous. A short iron and a long two-putt. But there is venom concealed by its natural beauty. If you think you can reach the heart of this sandy mountain, you can't afford to miss.

10th St Annes Old Links

317 yards, par 4

Turning to the back nine, we will come across several courses boasting their second inclusion. In the case of St Annes, featuring the returning hole of the first batch, it almost feels indulgent to include its 10th too. I toyed with the 16th, but thought two par 3s from the same course would risk a readers' revolt. Instead, the brilliantly bunkered 15th, its 11 bunkers, arranged as if to create an attractive pattern for the mathematically minded landing at the nearby aerodrome?

Well, I think the 10th deserves its place. It's not quite drivable, yet a good drive and incisive pitch might tame it. But this is easier said than done. Clean, tidy and borderline deferential, the pot bunkers elegantly snake across this hole. With two standing by on the left side of the drive, the main bunkers connect the right side of the fairway to the left of the green. Six of them sit in this meandering line – two creating the tapering point 240 yards from the tee, and the remaining four running in their diagonal echelon across to the left.

While the tee has been taken back as far as the road will allow, I don't think the hole would be enhanced by further extensions. As it is, a game of positional chess has developed. The ribbon of bunkers before the green, as well as the pitch and canter of the land, means the easy left-side lay-up leaves the hardest approach. Perhaps instead you should try and carry the two left-side fairway traps? Could be the play, just don't mess it up. What about the tricky shot down the right side? A more favourable approach, for sure. But be mindful of a drive scampering over the turf towards those waiting pots…

This hole tests thinking and placement. In a world where the sole rationale offered by the latest driver is greater distance, it rewards those who are capable of hitting it 'just far enough'.

11th Furness

435 yards, par 4

There were a range of viable options to choose from at Furness, but, most unfortunately, they again presented as a glut around the turn. This often-overlooked links on Walney Island starts from its elevated urban setting before tumbling some 15 metres down to true links terrain on the 3rd. It's at the 8th hole that over half this elevation is recovered.

I'm not often a fan of severely uphill holes, but this would be a reasonable exception. Twenty yards short and right of the green sits a WWII concrete pillbox. These fortified watching posts, manned by keen-eyed artillerymen as a last line of defence against an invading army, are still commonly found along Britain's coastline. Fortunately, an errant strike from a golf ball is the heaviest fire it was ever subjected to.

The hole I've put forth for the region's Eclectic 18 is Furness' 11th though. It's on the water's edge, as is the entire stretch from the 6th to 12th. Often on such a stretch, the golfer risks becoming desensitised to the wonderful flanking views. At Furness, it feels different. Perhaps it is the change in elevation, or the mix of hole types.

With a wide fairway, there is a lay-up bunker placed right in its middle. In the true traditional style, there is benefit for not shying away from the Pebble Beach which gives the hole its name (no relation). The green is one of the most interesting on the course. Large, bunkered asymmetrically and angled to favour the approach from the right. With the wind invariably whipping from this right side, there's a clear difference between having a helping wind over the right shoulder and hitting back out to sea and hoping for the best.

Furness wouldn't be able to furnish every position on this list, with holes of varying quality. But I reiterate the point I made in the main piece. It's one of England's most historic links courses and a course of true and genuine links credentials. It has often been omitted from other published collections of links courses, and I think it deserves far greater recognition than it gets.

12th Silecroft
125 yards, par 3

The eagle-eyed among you will have noticed I've featured a hole from nine-hole Silecroft on the Eclectic 18's back nine. In my mind, we enjoyed the unpretentious round enough to venture back out for a second loop. The result is the hole normally featuring as the 3rd becoming our 12th. I half toyed with including this hole into my collection of 'Fylde Threes'. With 10 bunkers encircling the putting surface, it shares some of the hallmarks. That group does tend to be slightly more polished than Silecroft – not that it would be fair to judge this small club on such gauche metrics.

While Silecroft is more clifftop than true links golf, this part of the course is the bit which comes closest to changing my mind. The beach is within chipping distance from the tee, and the strong helping wind brings the bunkers lurking beyond this green firmly into play.

13th Silloth-on-Solway
507 yards, par 5

Just as I had no intention of skipping over Silloth's wonderful 4th, the 13th was another hole I quickly committed to paper. During my time working at the architectural firm of Clayton, DeVries & Pont, I fondly remember many occasions walking fairways with the inimitable Mike Clayton. Clayts would argue a great par-5 was simply a brilliant drivable par-4, plus a good drive. In other words, it was all about the jeopardy of the second shot. The tee shot should be good enough to get you in position. It didn't need to be heavily bunkered or too penal. Get on the fairway, and then sweat over what to do next.

He might well have been describing this very hole. The drive is wide open. Anything under 300 yards that flies roughly straight will likely find short grass. But at this point the ground ceases to be level. A sharp ridge erupts from the landscape, the fairway beyond visible only in part – rising steadily on to a hog's-back green perched far higher than feels reasonable. After the relative comfort of the drive, the next shot is anything but. Every yard up the hole requires greater accuracy. Shunning the risk on the second and playing too tentative a lay-up means the tariff placed on hitting the green in regulation is equally elevated.

Bobby Jones said this game is played in the six inches between the ears. How right he was. This is a par 5 scarcely longer than some of the par 4s on this very list. There's no risk of finding the beach with an errant shot. Nor are there any bunkers. Realistically, there is more than enough space to play. Any capitulation on this hole will, almost certainly, be self-inflicted. Too tentative a climb towards the lofty summit.

14th St Bees
446 yards, par 4

Is this the most ingenious bell in British golf? It is certainly a one-off as far as I am concerned

Let's hope you held your nerve playing Silloth's 13th, maybe even returning a birdie four. Because at St Bees' 14th, there's every chance a bogey will follow. By some margin, I thought this was the best hole on the nine-hole course. Again, it's a hole normally played as the 5th, but it's so unlikely it will have been mastered on first playing, it will demand a second attempt.

St Bees is another pure clifftop course. Not that anyone, at least to my knowledge, has tried to claim it as anything else. After venturing up and over hills capable of wearing out mountain goats, this memorable hole runs along the very edge of the edge. The beach lies some 30 feet below, the sound of the crashing waves only just audible when I played – despite their proximity. But the views from this elevated vantage point are far reaching. It must be the nearest point to the Isle of Man – only 30 miles and due west from the 12th (5th) green.

This hole also boasts a unique distinction. One which I note here not to scoff or denigrate St Bees, but to revel in its ingenuity. The fairway sits slightly obscured from the tee and necessitates a bell to be struck to let waiting golfers know they're now free to drive. Rather than waste untold sums on polished brass bells, St Bees employs a claw hammer (now missing its claw), attached and ready to strike a perfectly modified (the base had been cut off) 'Shell Butagas' canister. 'Patent Pending – J.R. Stewart' was roughly scrawled across the ingenious solution. I hope the patent office duly licenses the design before clubs around the world follow suit.

15th Seascale
332 yards, par 4

After the strategic brilliance of the 3rd, Seascale winds and weaves through a varied landscape of rumpled ground and modest sand hills. At the 11th and 12th, we take a quick journey into the heart of the Sellafield Nuclear Plant itself.

High fences topped with razor wire line the edges of these holes. As if the many signs warning off would-be intruders (or drone operators) aren't enough, members of the armed Civil Nuclear Constabulary are on patrol. To my knowledge, it remains the only occasion I've stood over a three-foot putt in clear sight of an armed marksman.

While these holes certainly proved memorable, they aren't the great golf which quickly follows. I could have selected any of the holes from the 14th onwards. This one is a bunkerless par 5 running along another railway line. The ground in this part of the course is fabulous. This hole really has no right to fit into the space on offer. I would encourage particularly nerdy readers to seek out Seascale on 'Provisualizer' or the like.

The tee for the hole is hard against the railway line, and the hole turns almost straight back on the one just played, towards a green hemmed in between two tees. From here, it's another about turn to drive back along the self-same fairway – this time to a 16th green sat parallel again to the railway line. I would expect to be immediately dismissed if I suggested such a routing solution to a client, but it's a hole that's stuck with me. I think it might simply be because it captured the essence of great links golf so succinctly.

It is the curious. The unexpected. Quirky but thoroughly enjoyable, made great by the brilliant land on display. In fact, I might go so far as to say this small corner of this largely unknown course might have some of the most natural golfing contour in this volume. It also shows you can occasionally play yourself out of position, but with flair, great land and a healthy disregard for convention, you can probably get away with it.

16th Dunnerholme
138 yards, par 3

In Dunnerholme's first entry on this list, I alluded to the liberties I'd taken with the numbering of this imagined course. While I expect to be forgiven for including holes from nine-hole courses on the back nine of this list, I accept I'm pushing matters to include the 6th from 10-hole Dunnerholme as the 16th. Are you still with me? I hope so because this hole deserves your attention. I remember arriving at this tee and spending a full minute contemplating which direction to play.

From here, the green of the 7th is visible – albeit behind the stone wall discussed earlier. Equally visible are the parked cars and short terrace of cottages, standing at the base of the enormous Dunnerholme Rock. It's only while scanning the landscape in this direction that the very top of a fluttering flag is visible atop the rocky crag. As I study the unexpected scene, a line of white out-of-bounds posts can be spotted – winding their way up the almost-sheer face.

The card said 138 yards, but I remember hitting a full 4-iron to be sure I made the carry. I only narrowly made it. Reaching the top, I was relieved to find my ball safely aboard the round green – cut dead centre on top of this extraordinary geological feature.

17th Castletown
416 yards, par 4

A little like Silloth's 13th, Castletown's 17th was another of the first holes included on this list. It's brilliant. Absolutely brilliant.

CB Macdonald once wrote it is important to separate the 'art from the canvas'. In other words, the golfer should look beyond the landscape and see the intricacies and nuance of the architect's design. But when it comes to this hole, the canvas is its own masterpiece. The high point of the course, this is most definitely clifftop golf rather than the pure links enjoyed around Castletown's turn. Not that this technicality would be any reason to mark it down.

The waves crash white spray against the black, jagged basalt rocks. The wind drives salt-laden air across your face. Your ears are full of the cries of gannets and gulls. And beyond this edifying scene? A distant fairway.

From the back tee, it's almost 200 yards to reach the safety of the short grass – but who could not be inspired to turn their shoulders and not merely limp to the far side, but fly it with conviction? From the inevitability of the short grass, the rocky outcrops and fissures remain for the length of the hole. Perhaps 200 yards still to go.

The 17th at Castletown is one of the most famous sights in British Isles golf, a par 4 of unforgettable drama

When discussing Castletown's 6th hole, I reflected on the subtlety and technical elegance of Mackenzie Ross. Here, we must marvel at the tenacity and ambition of the same man. This is the architect who rebuilt Turnberry's Ailsa course – taking that course down to the jagged rocks around the iconic Lighthouse. Or the man who put Southerness's 12th green on the very edge of the Solway Firth. Both of those courses will be discussed at length in Volume 3 of this series. But for now, I will remember the rush of adrenaline which comes from standing on Castletown's 17th tee and applaud his dramatic collision of art and extraordinary canvas.

18th Royal Lytham & St Annes
410 yards, par 4

I've already borrowed Henry Longhurst's timeless praise of Tony Jacklin's fairway-splitting drive here. As Open Rota closing holes go, it must be one of the most memorable. Who can forget the heartbreak of Adam Scott's capitulation. Or Ballesteros almost holing from off this green in 1988?

It is a hole of significance. Capable of coronation or collapse. It also plays directly towards one of golf's most recognisable clubhouses. Royal Lytham's stately Victorian villa sits within gimme range from the back of this green. With the equally recognisable dormy house in clear view – it is as attractive an urban end to a round as you could ask for. But while these elements all add to the hole's charm, we must not forget that the hole really is a good one. No fewer than 17 bunkers line it. On the drive, the first and second set sit on the same diagonal angle. With golfers missing not equidistant left and right, but short right and long left, the golfer can't breathe easy until their ball is safely at rest above ground. If a bunker has been found, lay-up bunkers keep the mind focussed. As is the case throughout the round at Lytham, a mental lapse will quickly be punished.

Finally, attention might turn to the green itself. One of the largest on the course, it sits almost as a 'V-shape'. The bunkers running up each side of the green pinch tightly at the front, broadening slightly. This is a course so often firm and bouncy that, with a mid-iron in hand, the trade-off is between flying it far enough up the green to benefit from the width against the risk of a bounce long into Gary Player territory, who found himself in the flower beds around the clubhouse walls.

Lytham is a golf course of significance and, in my opinion, the perfect closing hole for our Eclectic 18 of what is a remarkably strong golfing region.

015/225

Royal Lytham & St Annes

George Lowe and Harry Colt created a links that richly rewards closer inspection. Among the subtler of the Open Championship venues, it is also the most heavily bunkered

TO the reader, I offer a conundrum. How can a course universally ranked in the world's top 100 be underrated? This is a course that has played host to 11 Open Championships, five Women's Opens, Walker Cups, Curtis Cups, Ryder Cups and more. It is as storied and distinguished as English golf gets. Respected, but not always loved.

Before we tackle this peculiar question, I think it is worth understanding exactly what the once-sleepy Fylde coast looked like at the turn of the 20th century.

Lytham & St Annes Golf Club was founded in 1886 but, with ongoing disputes over the lease of the land, only moved to this site in 1897. George Lowe, the club's professional, laid out the links on their new site and they have contentedly remained here ever since. These years and the impact of Mr Lowe are covered more comprehensively in the essay on St Annes Old Links (016/225) – so instead, we'll concern ourselves with the louder revolution ongoing.

For many years, holidaying at the seaside had been the preserve of the wealthy upper classes. In 1792, The Royal Hotel had been built in Hoylake to offer the wealthy merchants of Liverpool the chance to convalesce and benefit from the sea air. But a century later, a seaside holiday was open to all.

Towns including Brighton, Scarborough and Rhyl developed hotels, amusements, swimming baths and all manner of supporting infrastructure to become the preeminent destinations on the East, South and Welsh coasts respectively. As successful as these resorts were, there was one that stood above all others.

Its rise to dominance was rapid. Before the end of the 19th century, Blackpool boasted three piers, the vast Winter Gardens complex, the Pleasure Beach and, of course, the famous Blackpool Tower. The number of holidaymakers that could be accommodated swelled from 250,000 to 2,500,000 over the space of just 10 years.

But what made Blackpool most attractive was the price: finally affordable for working-class Victorians. I do wonder if this was another reason the early members of Lytham & St Annes, with the Blackpool Tower and Pleasure Beach both visible from their original links, eyed the growth with some trepidation.

Over the same time, the smaller towns of Lytham, Fairhaven and St Annes were also forging a reputation for seaside breaks. The key difference was in the clientele. Lytham St Annes, as the amalgamation of the two towns became, was seen as the 'posh' resort – the respectable alternative to Blackpool for the middle classes.

A reason cited for the creation of St Annes Old Links, essentially a splinter club from the original, was in response to the high rates of subscription that had priced out many of the keen local golfers. It offered golf at one fifth the cost of the gentrified Lytham & St Annes Club. With such extraordinary growth in such short periods of time, coupled with extreme seasonality – it must have been challenging to define the culture of these two young golf clubs.

But Lytham & St Annes flourished in the early years of the 20th century. By the time the Great War ended in 1919, Harry Colt was invited to make improvements to the course. To a greater or lesser degree, every hole was altered.

Lowe had built ridges and faux sand hills as part of his construction, but Colt focussed primarily on routing and strategy. New greens were built for the 3rd and 17th holes, but it was Lytham's bunkering

The par-3 9th green is encircled by bunkers – and these are among the very deepest pots on the links

Lytham's calling card is its bunkering – they are often asymmetrical and create fascinating strategic decisions

that received the most attention. Reports vary, but my interpretation of an old 1940s aerial show 261 bunkers across the course.

What strikes me most about this course is not the sheer quantity of bunkers, but their shape and arrangement. The fairways are wide and the greens large and shapely. Never circular, they are long and irregular in shape – the bunkering quite clearly designed to encourage play into them from one edge of the fairway or the other.

This was a hallmark of the great strategic architects of the era. A good drive wasn't simply 'straight down the middle', it required forethought and an understanding of the hole – it was likely to be an extremity of the fairway, opening up an angle to attack a pin that might otherwise be inaccessible from elsewhere. It was playable for the average golfer, as they plodded their way along safely away from the asymmetrically placed traps. But for the best players looking to shoot a number, they would have to take on risk on almost every shot to successfully do so.

Clearly the R&A agreed, announcing it would become the fourth English course to host the Open Championship in 1926. Lytham's *annus mirabilis* arrived with further accolades, King George V granting 'Royal' status to the club in May of that year. And so, Royal Lytham & St Annes Golf Club entered the golfing history books, the Championship capped off perfectly with the Champion Golfer for the ages claiming the job in dramatic fashion. More on that later. Colt made further changes to the links over the 1930s and it became a regular fixture on the Open Championship Rota from the 1950s. It quickly gained a reputation as one of golf's most challenging venues. The likes of Bobby Locke, Peter Thomson, Tony Jacklin, Gary Player, Ernie Els, David Duval and, most famously of all, Seve Ballesteros have all won Opens here.

It is an exacting test, often dismissed as austere in appearance and penal. A perennial criticism of those with only a passing understanding of links golf is

This 1940s aerial view shows over 260 bunkers – count them! – littered across the links

that: "Lytham can't be a links course; you can't see the sea from anywhere". The observation is entirely accurate, even if the conclusion is not.

The native sand, fine grasses and rumpling topography give this cerebral and self-assured links its sense of place. There are too many courses to name that have fine sea views but lack all other key ingredients.

When the site was first agreed upon, it was highly likely the sea would have been visible. The railway line and a handful of the grand Victorian villas did exist – but they were dotted around an open landscape of broken, sandy ground that connected the course to the sea. It was only the growth of the towns in the late 19th and early 20th centuries – including the construction of promenades and sea embankments – that isolated the links from the water's edge.

As to the penal nature of the bunkers, I believe this is more a question of interpretation than fact. Even now, with the bunker count reduced to a 'meagre' 168, there are still more here than at any other Open rota course – and 50 per cent more than even the Old Course at St Andrews. To those who visit the course once, find a handful of them and vow never to return – they will miss the essence of Lytham. Those who take the time to learn the course, visit more than once and slowly learn its secrets, will be rewarded.

Unfortunately, the wild and interesting shapes of the old bunkers have been lost. There is still an amount of variety, more than most modern rota courses, but generally they are small and rounded pot bunkers. So,

while the bunkers themselves might now be penal, the course retains a lot of its strategy. It is a thinking course where you must plot your way round.

If nothing else, it is still blessed with some wonderful holes.

Most unusually, the opening one is a par 3. No gentle warm up to the round here – a crisp and accurate iron shot is required from the outset. The drive on the 2nd is little easier – a long par 4 running along the railway line. The 3rd is similar – but would have been a greater test still in Colt's day. It's one of the only holes to have gained fairway bunkers. Historically, it was a true boundary hole. A centre-line bunker asked the questions on the drive: take on the railway line and be rewarded with a route into the well-guarded green.

"Those who take the time to learn the course, visit Lytham more than once and slowly learn its secrets, will be rewarded"

The 4th swings away from the railway and the 5th plays as a par 3 into the heart of the site. This is pure links land – rumpled and tumbling contours that sometimes get overlooked at Lytham.

The long 6th hole makes full use of this crumpled landscape. One of the more underrated holes on the course, a dogleg sweeps to the left and demands an inch-perfect approach by doing so. The ground contours buckle and lurch in the run-up to the green. Anything running up not on the perfect line will be thrown further off course. The green, which tapers dramatically from back left to front right, is a devilish one to find.

This long par 4 gives way to a long par 5, but we do notice a clear difference in fairway contour here. Rather than extraordinary irregularity, we see equal ridges and furrows – a throwback to the agricultural treatment of this particular parcel of land before the golf. Currently, there is a dense stand of deciduous woodland along the left side of the hole – an incongruous feature I believe is soon to change.

The 7th is a brute, but we quickly return to fine linksland again on the magnificent 8th hole. After driving parallel to the railway boundary again, we find it is the green complex that makes this hole so vexing. Three bunkers sit in the ridge that partially obscures the green – raised and with steep drop offs around the putting surface. The real trick is the bowl hiding between the ridge and green. Visually, it is a deceptive approach. Even for the player who knows the actual distance, the visual trickery of the design means you might struggle to trust it.

The 9th is another of the famous Fylde Threes – a par 3 so distinctive in style to this region. The bunkering is far more dignified and refined than the rugged and rustic images of old, but the essence of the hole is unchanged. A green with narrow front pushed up from the surrounding ground is ringed with seven deep pots.

The 10th has a sand hill eating into the left edge of the fairway, enough to push tee shots right – away from the ideal angle into this well protected green. Like many features at Lytham, it is subtle but effective. A marker post positioned down this left side reminds you where you should be aiming, but a clever little slope to the fairway beyond the hill will often catch a drive and send it left. Only a perfect drive will do.
The 11th is another very long par 5, but it leads to my favourite par 3 on the course. The 1st grabs the

The blind drive at the 16th – but this par 4 is actually one of the more straightforward holes on the closing stretch

attention, and the 9th lasts long in the memory, but I think 12 is probably the most intelligent of the lot. The green is almost 'L-shaped', a narrow tongue protruding short before the bulk of the green swings round to the right. The bunkers around this green feel placed, rather than simply dropped at random. They wrap around the left edge – leaving a small pair of spectacles guarding the back right portion of the green. When coupled with the run-offs around the green complex – they are ample protection.

Holes 13 through 15 are par 4s of increasing length, the 13th the most interesting and the 15th the most conventionally difficult. Focus on the immediate shot ahead is essential on this stretch, so much so that arrival on the 16th tee can almost creep up without notice.

In these essays, I try to focus on the clubs, their histories and elements that make them unique, as well as the courses themselves. Professional golf is often incidental, and I try not to dwell on it. However, it would be remiss to describe the closing three holes at Lytham without referencing some of the key events that have played out over them. For almost a century, they have made and broken prospective Open champions.

In 1979, it was the 16th hole that proved pivotal for a teenaged Seve Ballesteros. "I don't aim for the rough. It just goes there. My caddie tells me to close my eyes and hit it and maybe it goes in the fairway". This was Seve's response when asked why he persisted with his driver despite hitting just nine fairways through 72 holes. On the 16th hole of his final round, his slice came to rest under one of a handful of cars parked in the spare land between this and the 15th hole. Benefitting from a free drop, he pitched to 20 feet and rolled in the putt for a Seve-esque three. He went on to win his first major championship title by three strokes.

The 17th, as already alluded to, was immortalised by Bobby Jones. A fabulous hole to this day. The drive is broad for the shorter hitter but tapers dramatically further up, bunkered with sadistic enthusiasm. Fifteen bunkers line the hole now, but there were at least 19 in 1926.

Looking back down the 17th, one of many holes where Bobby Jones amazed the golfing world

Jones had started the day with poor fortune. Heading back to his hotel for lunch, he returned to play his final round without his player's identification. When the ticket officer failed to recognise him on re-entry, Jones elected to pay the spectator ticket price rather than embarrass him.

Having pulled his drive into a sandy wilderness down the left side of this penultimate hole, Jones played the shot of the tournament – a long iron that cleared the sand, gorse, dunes and all other trouble to nestle safely on the distant green that Jones would have been unable to see clearly. I do wonder if a sheepish ticket inspector watched the miracle shot on 17 or celebrations that soon followed. If he wasn't recognisable then, he must have been just a few months later as he became the first man to hold the Open and US Open titles in the same year.

Finally, the closing hole must rank as one of the best on the rota. It is certainly iconic – the imposing clubhouse and dormy house standing immediately behind the home green. Just the small matter of navigating the 17 bunkers that stand between this sanctuary and the tee.

Sometimes a Championship can come down to a single swing. In 2012, Adam Scott's drive trickled into a bunker here and his closing bogey handed the Claret Jug to Ernie Els. But in 1969, the pressure was on the shoulders of Tony Jacklin. With an 18-year drought in homegrown Open success, the pride of British golf was on the line. Legendary commentator Henry Longhurst sounded emotional as he described Jacklin's closing drive: "What a corker! He's driven it absolutely miles!"

If ever there were a course that has stood the test of time, this must surely be it. Since Colt's changes a century ago, the routing has hardly changed. There are very few Championship links courses where this is the case.

We are fortunate the early members knew what they wanted, and that they had the wherewithal to build it. If it was challenging to define the culture of this club at the turn of the 20th century, it is straightforward now. It is a club with a championship pedigree the equal of any other. A course that is always presented impeccably and requires thought and consideration to play well. It's not one that worries about its lack of views or strives for fairness. Lytham makes no apologies and nor should it. It has its own inimitable style, and it wears it well. LFTR

My 225 Club

Every British links that I visited on my self-imposed odyssey

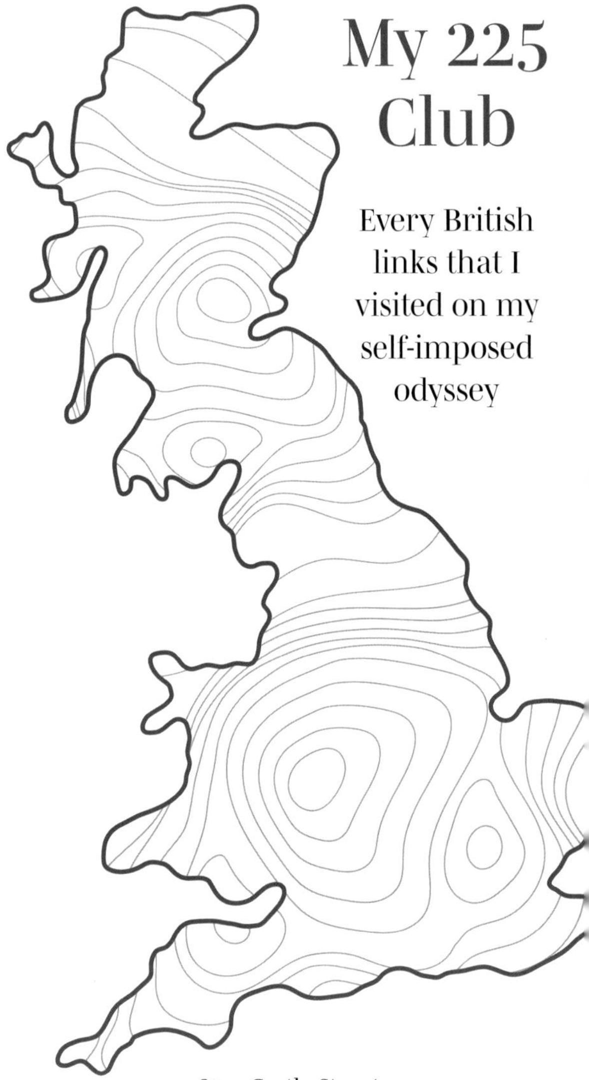

Volume 1

1 Royal Liverpool (Hoylake)
2 Leasowe
3 Wallasey
4 The Warren
5 West Lancs
6 Formby Ladies
7 Formby
8 Southport & Ainsdale
9 Hillside
10 Royal Birkdale
11 Southport Links (Muni)
12 Hesketh

Volume 2

13 Castletown
14 Fairhaven
15 Royal Lytham & St Annes
16 St Annes Old Links
17 Fleetwood
18 Furness
19 Dunnerholme
20 Silecroft
21 Seascale
22 St Bees
23 Maryport
24 Silloth on Solway

Volume 3

25 Powfoot
26 Southerness
27 St Medan
28 Stranraer
29 Wigtownshire County
30 Girvan
31 Turnberry KRTB
32 Turnberry Ailsa
33 Prestwick St Nicholas
34 Prestwick
35 Prestwick 12 holes

Volume 4

36 Royal Troon Portland
37 Royal Troon Old
38 Troon Municipal (Darley)
39 Troon Municipal (Lochgreen)
40 Kilmnarnock Barassie
41 Dundonald
42 Western Gailes
43 Glasgow
44 Irvine
45 West Kilbride
46 Shiskine

Volume 5

47 Machrihanish
48 Mach Dunes
49 Dunaverty
50 Carradale
51 Tarbert
52 Traigh
53 Colonsay
54 The Machrie
55 Isle of Iona
56 Tobermory
57 Isle of Skye

Volume 6

58 Ullapool
59 Gairloch
60 Durness
61 Barra
62 Askernish
63 Benbecula
64 Isle of Harris
65 Stornoway
66 Shetland
67 Asta
68 Whalsay

Volume 7

69 South Ronaldsay
70 Stromness
71 Orkney
72 Westray
73 Reay
74 Wick
75 Tarbat (Portmahomack)
76 Brora
77 Golspie
78 Royal Dornoch Struie
79 Royal Dornoch
80 Carnegie Club (Skibo Castle)

Volume 8

81 Tain
82 Fortrose & Rosemarkie
83 Castle Stuart
84 Nairn
85 Nairn Dunbar
86 Hopeman
87 Covesea
88 Moray New
89 Moray Old
90 Garmouth & Kingston
91 Spey Bay
92 Buckpool
93 Strathlene

Volume 9

94 Cullen
95 Duff House
96 Rosehearty
97 Fraserburgh

98 Inverallochy
99 Peterhead
100 Cruden Bay St Olaf
101 Cruden Bay
102 Newburgh on Ythan
103 Trump International
104 Murcar
105 Royal Aberdeen
106 Royal Aberdeen Silverburn

Volume 10

107 Kings Links
108 Nigg Bay
109 Stonehaven
110 Montrose 1562
111 Montrose Broomfield
112 Arbroath
113 Carnoustie Championship
114 Carnoustie Burnside
115 Carnoustie Buddon
116 Panmure
117 Monifieth Medal
118 Monifieth Ashludie

Volume 11

119 Scotscraig
120 St Andrews Jubilee
121 St Andrews Eden
122 St Andrews New
123 St Andrews Old
124 St Andrews Castle
125 St Andrews Strathtyrum
126 St Andrews Balgove
127 Kingsbarns
128 Crail GS
129 Anstruther
130 Elie
131 Dumbarnie
132 Lundin
133 Leven
134 Kinghorn

Volume 12

135 Musselburgh Old Links
136 Longniddry
137 Craigielaw
138 Kilspindie
139 Luffness New
140 Gullane 3
141 Gullane 2
142 Gullane 1
143 Gullane Kids
144 Muirfield
145 Renaissance
146 Archerfield Fidra
147 Archerfield Dirleton
148 North Berwick Kids
149 North Berwick
150 The Glen
151 Winterfield
152 Dunbar
153 Eyemouth

Volume 13

154 Berwick Upon Tweed (Magdalene)
155 Goswick
156 Seahouses
157 Dunstanburgh Castle
158 Alnmouth Village
159 Warkworth
160 Newbiggin by the Sea
161 Hartlepool
162 Seaton Carew
163 Cleveland
164 Scarborough South Cliff
165 Ganton
166 Seacroft

Volume 14

167 Hunstanton
168 Royal West Norfolk
169 Sherringham
170 Royal Cromer
171 Great Yarmouth & Caister
172 Aldeburgh
173 Felixstowe Ferry
174 North Foreland
175 Princes
176 Royal St Georges
177 Deal
178 Littlestone

Volume 15

179 Rye Jubilee
180 Rye
181 Littlehampton
182 Hayling
183 Barton on Sea
184 Isle of Purbeck
185 Dawlish Warren
186 Thurlestone
187 Mullion
188 Royal Jersey
189 La Moye
190 Royal Guernsey

Volume 16

191 West Cornwall
192 Perranporth
193 Newquay
194 Trevose
195 St Enodoc
196 Bude & North Cornwall
197 Royal North Devon
198 Saunton West
199 Saunton East
200 Minehead & West Somerset
201 Burnham & Berrow
202 Burnham & Berrow (Channel)
203 Weston Super Mare

Volume 17

204 Southerndown
205 Royal Porthcawl
206 Pyle & Kenfig
207 Swansea Bay
208 Pennard
209 Ashburnham
210 Tenby
211 Newport Links
212 Cardigan
213 Borth & Ynyslas
214 Aberdovey

Volume 18

215 Royal St Davids
216 Porthmadog
217 Pwlheli
218 Abersoch
219 Nefyn
220 Anglesey
221 Bull Bay
222 Conwy
223 North Wales
224 Rhyl
225 Prestatyn

016/225

St Annes Old Links

Unassuming on first encounter, the collection of short holes is quite exceptional. This is not a course to be under-estimated

WHEN links golf is your subject matter, 'Old' is a word that crops up from time to time. St Annes' Old Links, founded in 1901, is not necessarily one that should sport this title. Even considering just the 12 courses in this volume, only Fairhaven, Dunnerholme, Maryport and Silecroft were founded more recently. Hardly a justification for such a title.

But it was what happened here before 1901 that means the name is well deserved.

St Annes Old Links occupies an almost square piece of land. It may be relatively flat but the turf is exquisite

The Lytham & St Annes Golf Club, before it received its 'Royal' prefix, was founded on this site in 1886. For over a decade, the club grew in stature and significance – until such a point the short leases offered over the land became too great a concern for the club's membership. During what must have been a fractious negotiation, the club called the landlord's bluff and opted to acquire new land for golf rather than renew the existing lease. George Lowe, the club's professional, laid out the new course and Lytham & St Annes thrived. The membership grew and the subscription rates eventually priced out the working classes in the town. All the while, the 'Old Links' was left fallow and unleased.

On the 24th of June, 1901, 22 local businessmen decided the opportunity to take over the vacated lease was worth pursuing – and a new club on the old land was formed. George Lowe offered his design services free of charge and suggested a 9-hole course could be made ready in as little as two weeks' work for a pair of men. 'The Old Links Golf Club, St Annes on the Sea' was the proposed name, and the annual subscription should be one fifth that of the gentrified Lytham & St Annes Golf Club.

Lowe's nine holes at The Old Links were, of course, quite different from the course that had previously existed there – but the holes played today as the 10th and 17th holes remain from that 1886 course. They are the oldest holes in this Fylde Coast region still in play – and, to my mind, mean the 'Old' title of this club is fully warranted.

The short leases that drove Lytham & St Annes to move to their new site did continue to cause issues for the Old Links in their early years. An early vote of confidence in the club's future came from founding member and architect George Lowe in 1905.

Lowe was such a central figure in the establishment and popularisation of golf in this region I feel he justifies a brief digression. Before taking the role as professional when the Lytham & St Annes Golf Club was founded, he had served a 12-year apprenticeship with Hoylake's professional, Jack Morris. Jack was the nephew of Old Tom, visiting Hoylake alongside his father's assistant when he helped lay out the first links there in 1869. He suggested he might stay on as the professional and was encouraged to 'give it six months' by his father before returning to Scotland. Jack did a little better than that, staying in his role for over 60 years.

As well as tending to the course and offering lessons, a professional of standing would generate much of their income by advising on the layout and construction of new courses or by building clubs. Clearly, Lowe certainly had an eye for design – with St Annes Old Links, Lytham & St Annes and Birkdale among his architecture portfolio, but it was club-making where he invested most of his energies.

It is likely this fact that makes better sense of Lowe's decision to leave the steady employ of the prestigious Lytham & St Annes in favour of an unpaid position at the precarious St Annes Old Links. He was to act as professional and greenkeeper, but he was granted a workshop for a peppercorn rent.

Lowe's obituary claimed he went on to make and sell over 25,000 golf clubs over his career, an extraordinary number. He pioneered new technologies, as the first person to patent the concept of 'matched sets' of irons – and even a 'full faced' mashie. He even designed a club with the face set ahead of the shaft, the tonic of Victorian golfers with a case of the shanks.

Ultimately, George Lowe was a man often overlooked by history, but one who contributed an extraordinary amount to help drive the game forwards during its 'boom' years.

Whether Lowe's relocation to the Old Links helped drive the club forward or not is unclear, but by 1909 a 40-year lease had been signed for 90 acres of land – allowing the club to finally take a long-term approach to the development of the links.

Lowe worked with the 1902 Open Champion Sandy Herd to propose an extension of the course from nine holes to an 18-hole layout. Soon after, a new clubhouse was commissioned, opening in 1911.
It was a period that defined the next century of St Annes Old Links. The course retains many of the holes and changes Lowe and Herd proposed, and the clubhouse is still this impressive Victorian building – grand, yet without pretension. Visible from almost every hole, and a parallel to the club and indeed course itself.

The excellent par-3 16th at St Annes Old Links, a Fylde Three before two par-5s to finish

The links is generally flat. There are few dunes, but no shortage of bunkers or vexing run offs and ridges. It's a course that I think improves with repeat plays but has stand-out moments that will impress even on a cursory visit.

The front nine winds in a loop along the 'inland' half of the site. The course never ventures quite to the water, separated by a railway line and road from the beach – but the westerly section of the site is the 'linksier' portion.

The 1st and 6th greens are almost a double green – just the cut height of the apron separating the putting surfaces here. The 3rd is a devilishly bunkered par 3 tucked and sets the early standard for one of the best collections of par 3s in the region.

The 5th and 6th are back-to-back par 5s, a feature you rarely come across – but one repeated later in the same round on holes 17 & 18. But among the good holes of the front 9, the highlight without question is the famous 9th hole.

A par 3 playing back towards the clubhouse, the green is long and narrow – set naturally at the foot of encircling sand dunes. It is the biggest land movement on the course, and it utilised in one of the most memorable ways possible.

The hole, called 'The Cannon', is said to have so impressed Bobby Jones – visiting before his maiden Open Championship victory at Lytham in 1926, described it as 'difficult to improve upon'. He was said to have staked out the measurements of the green and bunkers – making notes for future reference.

Apart from the stately 10th, with all its historical pedigree, the back nine really comes into its own from the 13th, a par 3 that on another course would be a standout, before one of the most intimidatingly bunkered approaches to the par-4 15th. No fewer than eleven bunkers defend his hole. Normally, I would question if such excess were necessary – so often the over-bunkering a hole is the last resort of

The famous par-3 9th – The Cannon – with its incredible green site would grace any links on the Open Championship rota

Difficult to improve upon'. Who would argue with this assessment of the famous 9th from Bobby Jones?

one without real identity or clarity of strategy. But here, it is the character of the hole. The bunkers on the approach sit beautifully in the landscape – a series of swales and hollows filled with sand to confuse and intimidate the player.

The reward for surviving 15 is the equally intimidating 16th hole. 'Keepers Trap' is the appropriate name for this par 3, an upturned green wearing a delicate necklace of pot bunkers. Rather than feeling contrived, it sits innocently against the backdrop of sand hills beyond. It is a hole type that seems to feature on several of the courses in this part of England, but rarely seen elsewhere. The 5th at Royal North Devon is one that comes to mind, but there are clear examples of this style of hole at nearby Royal Lytham, Fleetwood, and Fairhaven.

The 17th, another of the original Lytham & St Annes holes from 1886, has been stretched to a gargantuan 621-yard par 5 – but provides enough challenge from the members' tees. With the railway track stretching down the right side, a small dune ridge cutting through the fairway beyond the drive is the less obvious hazard. It is nothing like 'The Gumbleys' featured in Volume 1 at Southport & Ainsdale (another course originally laid out by George Lowe). There, the bisecting is so pronounced it imprints in your memory long after the round. Here, the ridge is rather subtle. A few feet high, it does just enough to obscure the view of the green from the left side of the fairway – the natural place a good drive might be expected to finish. Playing a long approach to a green that can't be seen, especially at such a key point of the round, inevitably leads to an uncomfortable second shot here. The challenge doesn't have to be overblown, just enough to influence your approach to the hole over repeat plays – often a hallmark of restrained and intelligent design.

If 17 is a bit of brawn, 18 is all brain, and by some margin, the shortest par 5 on the course. Rather than see this as a weakness, the savvy members of the Old Links understand that the chance to go for triumph, risking disaster at the same time, is the ultimate challenge of a closing hole. The same risk of the boundary lurks down the right edge, but the challenge now is the accuracy required to run the ball into the green in two when the ground is hard and running. Short of the green, a diagonal ridge cuts down the fairway. Anything running over this (or, even worse, landing on its down-slope) will kick the ball on and left – either ending in or behind the greenside bunkers that protect this side. Holding the green requires a deft touch, carrying far enough to find the flat run up to the green beyond this canny ridge.

An average round can be turned into a great one with a strong finish, just as a good one can be thrown away with a couple of ill-conceived swings.

I do always wonder what visiting golfers make of this links as they retire to the clubhouse to reflect. My guess is it passes many of them by. They might wonder why a course from 1901 is considered 'Old'. They might wonder why it is not quite as grand nor as polished as the Royal club two miles down the road. They might think the flat landscape was less than they were expecting and, par 3s aside, it was a course they found difficult rather than enjoyable and memorable.

Personally, I think that misses the point of the Old Links. In many ways, it was founded to be something very different to Lytham & St Annes. It was founded by visionary golfers happy to shoulder a financial risk to create a good-value club that welcomed everyone who loves the game of golf, not just those with deep enough pockets. I think they created a course that serves a diverse and passionate membership still. And for me, it's a course that gets better with each visit, revealing its strategies and secrets at its own pace. LFTR

017/225

Fleetwood

This Lancashire links has had multiple homes but can lay a legitimate claim to being the oldest golf club in England

IF you were to ask the well-informed golfer which is the oldest seaside course in England, they would likely say 'Westward Ho!'. Founded in 1864, their links is better known as Royal North Devon and proudly calls itself the 'cradle of English golf'. Others might point to the likes of Royal Blackheath, where club records stretch back over 400 years, albeit with gaps variously throughout the centuries. But rarely is the name of Fleetwood thrown into the mix.

Compared to these dignitaries of golfing history, the modern links of Fleetwood is but a youth – not yet 100 years old. This course was laid out in 1932 by the professional of Blackpool Golf Club, Jack Steer, but this isn't Fleetwood's full story. Before looking at the present course, I hope you might indulge a trip further back in time.

The 1932 links is not the first to have been laid out in Fleetwood. In fact, this modest club has a particularly rich history. None of the earlier versions seemed to last longer than a few years, and the courses the club played over were similarly changeable. 1910, 1903 and 1893 are three other dawns, but there is another earlier genesis which is significant enough to mention. It was only a six year spell, but from 1861 to 1867, the first version of Fleetwood Golf Club has legitimate claim to be one of the oldest in England. Upon reading this, I thought there must have been a record-keeping error. Why would one of English golf's first outposts be in this quiet corner of Lancashire?

Well, in this era, Lancashire was anything but quiet. With coal and water in plentiful local supply, as well as raw cotton arriving in the nearby port of Liverpool, Lancashire became known as 'cottonopolis'. By the mid-1850s, over 30 per cent of the world's cotton fabric came from the region, which was responsible for over half of Britain's global exports.

With such rapid growth in industry came investment in infrastructure. First, the canal, but soon after the railway. Historians know how significant the railway became in the proliferation of courses, but it was a shortcoming of the line that we can thank here.

Fleetwood, a genuine links, is separated from the Irish Sea by the width of a coastal wall

The Lake District, full of its mountains and eponymous lakes, had provided a natural barrier between England and Scotland. The two rail networks were not connected. The quickest route was to catch a train from London's Euston station and travel by rail to Fleetwood. From this seaside port, a ferry could be caught to Ardrossan before an onward train into Glasgow.

To allow Fleetwood to benefit from this route, the local landowner built the North Euston Hotel. A grand structure, it would allow the weary travellers on this long route to spend a night in luxury before catching the onward ferry the following morning. Engineering ultimately prevailed and a direct line between the two cities was laid. As the visitors dried up, the expansive North Euston Hotel was a natural victim. It was sold on to the War Office in 1860, who relocated their School of Musketry to the building.

With the North Euston backing on to sandy links land, it didn't take long for the Scottish officers to suggest they should craft a rudimentary course. Clubs and balls were purchased from St Andrews and shipped down to Fleetwood and a competition was dutifully fought in November 1861.The victors were Captain Waldy and Lieutenant Walker. The connection to the game for founding Fleetwood member Lieutenant Walker is straightforward: Arthur Campbell-Walker was a native Scot, raised in Carnoustie country. He joined the 79th Regiment of the British Army, The Queen's Own Cameron Highlanders – based in Inverness. He fought in the Crimean War and in the Indian Uprising of 1857, returning to England as an expert in the entirely modern rifle. He wrote books on the subject and taught at the Musketry School.

Captain Waldy's connection with the game is less clear. He was a member of the 46th Regiment, based in south Devon in an area with no known golf before the match in question. He too was decorated for his part in the Crimean War, and had risen quickly through the ranks of his regiment. During Waldy's impressive rise through the regiment, his Colonel is someone who most certainly had a firm affinity with golf. General John Hamilton Dalrymple, the 8th Earl of Stair, has a name familiar to golfers of East Lothian. A true aristocratic family of Scotland, the Hamilton-Dalrymple have a strong connection to the game. It was this family that gifted the land of North Berwick's West Links to the club, and it is a name that repeats through past captains of the Honourable Company of Edinburgh Golfers. It is pure conjecture on my part, but perhaps Captain Waldy derived his

"Fleetwood's front nine takes the long way around the boundary of the site before returning to the clubhouse"

interest in the Scottish game from his commanding officer.

There is a parallel here to the foundation of another of England's oldest clubs, Royal Wimbledon. In 1864, it was Scottish members of the London Scottish Rifle Volunteer Corps based near Wimbledon Common who formed the London Scottish Golf Club, becoming Royal Wimbledon Golf Club in the early 20th century.

The school was relocated in 1867 to Hythe, on the south coast, and Fleetwood Golf Club did not continue. It remained an interesting footnote to the proliferation of the game in England, forgotten until a new club was founded again in 1893. Again, it did not last long. In 1910, the club merged with Knott End Golf Club and co-existed for several years before going their separate ways. Only then was Fleetwood laid out over the site it occupies today. The bunkering of the modern course is a little overzealous, some 122 of them scattered across subtly undulating ground. Separated from the sea by a recently constructed sea wall, there is little doubt it remains a links. The wind whipping across the Irish Sea was an unrelenting adversary when I played.

The routing makes full use of this challenge, changing direction regularly enough to never play a run of holes with the same wind. It achieves this with a recognisable and intelligent routing. From the clubhouse in the centre of the property, the front nine takes the long way around the boundary of the site before returning to the house. The second nine winds its way through the 'inner' land confined by it.

The same pair of loops had been employed just a few miles down the coast during Fairhaven's 1924 rebuild. But architecture afficionados will recognise this routing from Muirfield. The outer and inner loops there are famous the world over. Jack Steer, Fleetwood's architect from the 1932 course, happened to work alongside James Braid on Fairhaven's 1924 rebuild. Again, we enter conjecture, but I do wonder if inspiration for this routing came from the East Lothian classic. Braid was clearly a great disciple, naming his second son Harry Muirfield Braid.

However Fleetwood's routing came to be, it's a wonderful feature of this often overlooked course. Visit the clubhouse and there is virtually no reference to their tenuous claim as one of the oldest golf courses in England. Their priorities seemed clear. This is a members' club and they are more concerned with looking after the local golfers who are proud to call the club home. LFTR

DURING my 'day job' working as a golf course architect, I am acutely aware I spend more time than most obsessing over the things under the surface that might lead to good golf. Around the coast, it's often obvious if a site would be sandy or not. Often, and especially in Britain, any undeveloped dune system is likely protected for ecological purposes. But sites that look like they're heavy soils (and would require massive work to make them suitable for good golf) can often be misleading.

Certain plants and vegetation, different colours of the grasses, the amount of moisture in areas – they could all be signs that a vein of sand lurks below the surface. Sometimes with bated breath, a hole is dug. The top layer will likely be dark – full of years of organic decay. But, if we are lucky, there might be a glimpse of gold beneath.

Like the prospectors who used to sieve the river sediment in search of a glint that might change their fortunes, finding sand on site could be the difference between a site being viable for golf or not. As I drove through the old warehouses and redeveloped factory buildings of Barrow-in-Furness, my mind wandered to the other things that have been found underground that can lead to a new golf course.

Founded in 1872, Furness Golf Club is another of England's ancients. We must remember that the only other existing links in England at the time were Westward Ho! (Royal North Devon, 1864), Hoylake (Royal Liverpool, 1869) and Alnmouth Village (1869). This was before the golf boom toward the end of the 19th century when golf was still a little-known game played primarily by the Scots.

The unmistakeable links fairways prove Furness is the real deal

018/225

Furness

This is yet another English links that we have the Scots to thank for – who brought the game with them when they came south to work. Not many make the journey to this corner of Cumbria but it is well worth the effort

So, what was the catalyst for Furness's formation? Barrow is old. Neolithic, in fact. The Romans were here, and a hoard of Viking gold found in recent years suggests they were too. But, in the mid-19th century, it was little more than a minor port. There were fewer than 10,000 people living in the wider area by 1861 and yet, 10 years later, this number had doubled.

It was a discovery from an iron prospector, Henry Schneider, which set about this transformation. Schneider found deposits of iron ore in the area. He organized the Furness Railway to be constructed, allowing the mines that were quickly dug to transport their product throughout the British Empire.

But soon the hematite iron oxide Schneider had found was being used to create not just pig iron, but steel. A Bessemer steel plant was built in 1865 and soon grew to create the Barrow Hematite Steel Company Limited. With a railway and a dock on hand, the operation grew rapidly – the population quickly doubling again so that, by 1881, it stood at almost 50,000.

Of the workers brought in to work in these steel mills, many were Scots. By the end of the 19th century – when Barrow was the biggest steel producer in the world – it was believed there were more native Scots residing here than in any other part of England. Naturally, it would make sense that some of these Scottish workers would bring their game with them, and so they did.

Furness Golf Club was founded by workers originally hailing from Dundee, working not in the steel mill but a flax mill which had been built nearby to benefit from the population boom of this industrial town.

It started as a makeshift six-hole course along Biggar Bank, likely just to the south of the current course.

Nine holes were then laid out on the present site and extended to 18 as the game's popularity really took hold.

The links isn't technically in Barrow, but on Walney Island. At the height of Barrow's industry, this was the far side of the dock – accessible only by a ferry and, most likely, a reprieve amid nature from the smog and chaos of the town itself. In 1908, Walney Island was connected to Barrow by the Jubilee Bridge and a new clubhouse was commissioned soon after. As war broke out in 1914, Barrow became of even greater strategic importance for the war effort. The production of steel was of national importance, and a shipbuilding industry flourished in the town. Particularly, submarines and zeppelin-style airships. These airships were constructed in a purpose built shed immediately adjacent to the golf course.

As might be expected for such a strategically important town, the defensive fortifications were

How can it be that a links with vistas like this is so routinely overlooked by curious golfers visiting the north west?

enormous. A minefield occupied most of the golf course, and airships were even being constructed on what in peace time had been the 5th fairway. Throughout, golf continued – albeit on a somewhat scaled-down four-hole course.

The shipbuilding only grew after the war, and Barrow continued to thrive. Vickers Boat Yard was one of the biggest shipbuilders in the country, building warships and submarines for the British Navy. HMS Invincible and all of Britain's Vanguard class submarines came from Barrow – which is still the only place in the UK capable of making and servicing nuclear-powered submarines.

Now, the hematite is used and BAE Systems, who operate the boat yard, employ a fraction of the people who once worked here at the town's peak.

But those raw materials found here have left a legacy of golf. The links of Furness are little known and regularly overlooked. They do not feature in Peper and Campbell's 'definitive' list of the 246 links courses of the world as catalogued in their 'True Links' book. If you search for reviews of the course online, few will come up.

I didn't really know what to expect when I drove the van over the Jubilee Bridge to Walney Island on my visit. The course is not impressive on first site, a relatively flat area with a few too many holes cramped over it.

But, from the inauspicious start, my opinion quickly changed. Cresting the hill after the 2nd green, the short par-4 3rd hole is one that will put a smile on any face. The land cascades and tumbles down the hill with the kind of contours reserved only for true links golf.

The rest of the golf on this opening stretch is perfectly pleasant, but it is at the 6th hole – where we turn away from the residential canvas that flanks the right side of the opening holes and directly towards the sea – where the course moves up a gear.

From the 7th to the 12th, we play one hole after another along the water's edge. The ground is delightful – rugged and rough maybe, but full of life and quirk. The views as we navigate this stretch are beautiful.

Every so often we encounter another relic from the area's many war defences as a reminder of times past. For example, the 8th green has an old concrete gun turret still defending the short right miss. Fortunately, it is no longer manned.

A particular favourite on this run is the 10th hole, the final par 3. A beautiful green sits ready to accept only the best long iron – one which has avoided the bunkers which look by far the most likely outcome of any tee shot.

The 11th is the first in a series of eight successive par fours to complete the round, albeit one that is only a few yards short of being classed as a par 5. It has the length, the views, and the contour to be a contender for the best hole on the course.

After the 12th, we turn away from the coast and venture inland for the remainder of the round. The views might be reduced, but the quality of the golf isn't. The 13th relies on great craters and run offs down the left side of the hole for its drama and challenge.

The 16th is another drivable par 4. Short and, at first glance, innocuous enough to tempt you into going for it, this is a hole bunkered well enough to make you regret that decision very soon after.

Is Furness worth visiting? Well, it depends. Barrow-in-Furness has been referred to as the 'longest cul-de-sac in England'. The far end of the Furness peninsula, it is not somewhere you pass by. For the mainstream, I can understand why it is perhaps a bridge too far. But there will be no shortage of links lovers holidaying in the Lake District who should make the journey.

This is a proper links with proper pedigree. Drive over the bridge to Walney Island as the sun dips towards the horizon line and I heartily believe that, like me, you will wonder why this historic links is so often overlooked. LFTR

Those who make the journey to Furness are rewarded with classic seaside golf and holes that run alongside the water

019/225

Dunnerholme

Close to Ulverston at the southernmost tip of the English Lake District is this charming oddity – a 10-hole course with barely a bunker but certainly no shortage of natural defences

WHAT makes a 'proper' golf course? Does it have to be par 72? With four par-5s and four par-3s? Well, if that were the criteria you could throw out over half of the links courses of Great Britain. Does it need to have manicured greens and tightly cut fairways? Some of those featured later in this series will certainly fail on that metric. Perhaps it must be 18 holes? Or perhaps we could grudgingly include the odd 9 holer. Well, this would rule Dunnerholme out – the only 10-hole course I visited on my travels.

Missing out Dunnerholme was a mistake I nearly made myself. Very little has been written about this quirky little course, hidden away on the north edge of the Furness Peninsula. It was another absent from the 'True Links' book that had provided the starting point for my own research. Message boards from the golfing equivalent of the Dark Web had provided more and Twitter (as it was once called!) really helped to round out the rest. But Dunnerholme was absent from my first list.

It was as I overzealously navigated our van around a sharp right-angled bend that I spotted a discreet road sign: 'Dunnerholme Golf Club'. I knew the sign was also pointing in the rough direction of the beach, so I had a growing niggle in my stomach that we had driven past somewhere we shouldn't have. My curiosity finally getting the better of me, I pulled over and consulted Google Maps – the real hero of the journey. The anxiety was well placed. It looked good, well worthy of a visit.

Fortunately, this was the height of summer, and there was no shortage of light to make it round the course. The opening hole, though, did make me question whether it warranted the U-turn. It was on interesting land, playing along a hog back fairway, but it was soft and lush underfoot.

Finding the 2nd tee requires a bit of orienteering – over the access road, around the edge of the neighbouring caravan site and through a gap in the trees – arriving on the edge of the Duddon Channel.

The green at the remarkable par-3 5th is approached from the foot of the cliff that defends it. Be sure to club up

The holes ahead curve gently around the sandy beach, with an imposing hill in the near distance that looks as if it has at some time been decapitated. This is Dunnerholme Rock, a dominating feature that plays more than a visual role.

Across the estuary, The Black Combe stands like a solitary outcast – just removed from the huddle of mountains and glens that comprise England's Lake District National Park. It really is a spectacular backdrop for golf.

The holes that follow aren't bad either. The 2nd quickly justified its late inclusion to the tour, a fairway rumpled and bounding with the links character I'd hoped for. There are just two bunkers at Dunnerholme. Instead the main hazards in this portion of the course are ditches. They have been intelligently cut, running across the fairways diagonally at points that are – undoubtedly by design – the exact points you might otherwise hope to play to.

The par-3 4th hole is cut through stands of gorse – the firm ground ready to deflect any ball not accurate enough to hold a large, undulating green running away from you. The 5th is strong – a long par 4 with gorse flanking the left side and a rumpled fairway cut through by a lane and bank just short of the green.

The 6th tee was straightforward to locate, but the green less so: 138 yards, the scorecard read. I hadn't walked past a green while approaching the 5th and couldn't see anything straight ahead. There was a green off to the right, but far further than the yardage on the card suggested.

The tee almost sat in the shadow of the giant Dunnerholme Rock, and considering its near sheer face, I realised this was the only remaining option. Lo and behold, a striped marker post stood at the top of the near vertical edifice. I played the shot more like 200 than 138 and was glad I did. A breathless walk up the path cut round the edge of the stone, and I

found my ball had only just made the climb. The green cut atop the rock is basic, but the challenge is joyous. From this vantage point, the view, beautiful from the 2nd tee, was utterly sensational. I'm sure I'm not alone in finding a childlike buzz in hitting a ball up or off such a dramatic feature, so I was delighted to find the 7th tee on top of the rock too.

As much fun as the 6th is, the 7th must be the best hole on the course. Playing back inland, the drive from such an elevated height to the fairway far below is well and truly at the mercy of the wind. A small stone cottage sits below the tee, and I think one drive too many has found its way onto the roof. The tee used most often now is a little to the side.

With the drive being pure fun, the approach requires a deft touch. This time, it is an old stone wall that cuts diagonally in front of the green. Not unlike the famous Pit at North Berwick, there is the potential to make a real mess of a hole that should be straightforward on paper.

Cris-crossing streams that complicate drives and approaches are a recurring theme at Dunnerholme

Holes 8 and 9 are enjoyable but serve more to return us from our mountaineering adventures. The 10th presents one last dose of quirk. The fairway climbs steeply up and over a ridge, the green blind beyond. The clubhouse, however, is not blind. It sits immediately to the right of the fairway, a visceral reminder to not leak one right. If the carry to the top can be made, there's a good chance a ball will run down to the waiting green below. Again, this is a hole that I can say with conviction you won't find elsewhere.

And that was my defining memory of Dunnerholme. Eccentric holes, utterly unique. Some of them are pleasant but little more, but some put a smile on my face whenever I think back to them. I don't know whether you could call Dunnerholme a 'proper' course or not, but I don't think it cares much for convention anyway. LFTR

020/225

Silecroft

A taste of quintessential Scottish village golf on the Cumbrian coast

THERE is something quite soulful about putting a modest green fee into an envelope and posting it into an honesty box. It's an experience you'll come across more readily in Scotland than England, where golf is just part and parcel of the local culture. A 9-hole course, basic in design and presentation, is commonplace. Not something viewed as second rate, but simply a community asset where the locals can enjoy a few holes when the mood takes them.

Silecroft is an example of the same on the southwest Cumbrian coast. It's not a renowned golfing destination. There is no shortage of tourists to the Lake District, but few of them venture far enough off the M6 motorway to find their way to the coast. Therefore, the 9 holes of Silecroft play a similar role to those community courses of Scotland.

Silecroft is absent from the True Links book that provided the initial list of my links courses, but I read some debate in the dark depths of an architectural message board and thought it should feature on the tour. I must admit, I'm glad I did include it.

It's not links golf, but the setting atop the cliffs was beautiful on the summer's evening I visited. The wind encouraged the waves to chase and crash below, and we were just able to make out the distant shape of the Isle of Man jutting above the horizon.

Inland, the flat land of the course continues over a patchwork of agricultural fields, a valley providing a long view east. But the dominating feature on the landscape is undoubtedly Black Combe – the grand feature of this southwest corner of the Lake District National Park. Not as tall as the main mountains and fells of the Park, the stark contrast between it and the flat land it sits in provides a dramatic juxtaposition.

The course at Silecroft offers more of this. Flat and generally with little topographical interest, it is the views that create much of the interest here. There are some interesting greens. Just enough slope and character to enhance the round. It is probably the par-3 3rd hole that serves as the most memorable moment. It's not the length but the 10 (yes, ten) bunkers encircling the green that provide the interest here. It might be a bit of a novelty, but it certainly does leave Silecroft with a hole that sticks in the mind.

For a course with no pretentions, it would be unfair for me to judge it as something it does not claim to be. It is a local course where visiting golfers are welcome to play for a modest green fee posted into an honesty box. A style of golf with the true spirit of the Scottish game. LFTR

It is hard not to embrace the setting of Silecroft, a 9-hole course on the clifftops of Cumbria

INTERESTINGLY, there are four courses played on this tour that have a truly industrial backdrop. Two are on the west coast and two on the east, all four with roughly the same latitude. On the east, Seaton Carew has the backdrop of Hartlepool Power Station and Cleveland had, at least until it was very recently demolished, the expansive Redcar Steel Works.

Featured in this volume, Silloth on Solway has an old flour mill immediately adjacent to the course. But none of these can compete with Seascale's neighbour. Sellafield is Europe's largest nuclear facility, covering more than 650 acres. Originally, it was built as a munitions plant during the Second World War but was converted to a nuclear power station after hostilities ended – serving this role for over 60 years before entering a decommissioning phase.

Golfers visiting these courses always make comment on these incongruous amalgams of steel and concrete – often saying how they detract from an otherwise picturesque setting. Personally, I quite like them. Not for everyday life perhaps, but occasionally, it is interesting to see the brutal juxtaposition of sand hills and science. Two unlikely bedfellows, so completely at odds with one another they bring almost a novelty value.

It is worth mentioning, as I think Sellafield is almost the elephant in the room when playing golf at Seascale. With the barbed wire fencing, armed police visible on patrol and the slight unease of looking on at its four nuclear reactors – it isn't something that can be ignored.

But I think we've covered it well enough, as the golf at Seascale deserves mention purely on its own merit. It certainly came first. If nuclear energy didn't arrive until the 1940s, golf had a 50-year head start here.

In 1893, Willie Campbell laid out nine holes on the site. Campbell, from the famous golfing town of Musselburgh, was something of a child prodigy. At the age of 13, he defeated Bob Ferguson – one of only four

We have to wait until reaching the 13th to access Seascale's lower level and the chance to play amid this glorious linksland

021/225

Seascale

Laid out on three distinct tiers, and shaped by three architects, this is a links that is remrkably rich in character and has a wonderful mixture of holes – from the long to the very short

people to win three successive Open Championships – in a high-profile match. Such was Campbell's popularity, one particularly wealthy admirer bet £30,000 that no one in the world would be able to beat him. Campbell spent six years playing anyone who would dare challenge him and won every time. Soon after Seascale was opened, Campbell moved to the United States – becoming the first professional at The Country Club in Brookline and moving to Myopia Hunt Club before his untimely death at the age of just 38.

In 1899, George Lowe – who readers of the St Annes Old Links piece will remember well – was invited to build nine more holes. This is the course played until further revisions were made by the great Harry Colt in 1932 – and his intelligent design is entirely evident today.

Seascale starts slowly, the 1st a gentle opener and the 2nd a little bit of bunkering away from being a good boundary hole. The 3rd is where it really gets going, a dogleg of almost 90 degrees around a small turf 'cop', with a field of grazing sheep beyond it. It was hard to not be reminded of my native Hoylake by this pastoral take on our opening hole.

The 4th and 5th play back and forth over a rumpled ridge system in the middle of the property – the 4th as a blind drive over the top and the 5th as a

The short 10th is a glorious links par 3 – the intrigue provided by a meandering stream and a fascinating green shape

good length par-3 with the green banked into it. The 6th and 7th made me wonder if they were contributions of George Lowe, a pair of back-to-back par 5s reminiscent of those at St Annes. The 8th is a good par-3 but, for me, the 9th must be the highlight of this side.

There is a tiger tee pushed all the way back on this hole, but if a tee is well selected here, it's a drive that poses a fabulous question. The fairway kicks quite dramatically from left to right, a significant drop separating the first and second half. If an accurate drive can be played to the end of the higher left edge, it leaves a clear view straight down to the green beyond. The right route requires a proper hit – or else risk leaving challenging blind approach from some rather gnarly rough. No bunkers are required here, the land provides more than adequate test – but there is a stream that runs long right of the green. It is not a hole to lose concentration on.

This same stream then meanders artfully in front of the beautiful 10th green. This is my favourite par-3 here at Seascale, short – but with a fabulously interesting green. The 11th and 12th are the holes probably too often remembered for the wrong reasons. They are the pair that play down a cul-de-

The par-5 14th runs parallel to the railway line before the 15th – outrageously – calls for a drive back over the previous green

sac almost into Sellafield itself. I found it to be an odd sensation and happily admit feeling a sense of relief as I putted out on the 12th green and turned my back on the facility. The holes themselves also lack a little of the links character that had been so evident up to that point but are bunkered well and under different circumstances would be well thought of.

The 13th is a nice par 3 but the run that follows it is nothing short of excellent.

The 14th is a short par 5 running parallel to the railway tracks down the right side. Comfortably reachable in two, there are no bunkers here to dissuade you from trying – but enough humps and hollows to make straightforward recovery from a failed attempt anything but a certainty.

The 15th is somewhat of a curiosity. Shoehorned in between 14 and 16, the tee is banked against the railway line and the drive is back over the 14th green. It feels as if you're playing to the 16th fairway rather than one for this hole. But rather than being a victim of this, I found it to be one of my favourites. Again, it shows the merits of great land and a truly beautiful green complex.

The 16th is the pick of the bunch. A long par 4, it stretches over rollicking links land towards a distant green tucked mischievously behind a pair of dunes. Anyone going for the green in regulation must navigate this intelligent feature to do so successfully. I offer a little more narrative on why I think it's such an interesting hole in 'My Favourite Holes' section earlier in this volume.

Seascale is a links laid out over three different levels. The opening holes start high, adjacent to the agricultural land, before falling to the middle tier and navigating the beautiful ridges that characterise the middle of the front nine. The section from 13 onwards, the strongest of the course, is on the lowest level. Here, the views that were previously enjoyed over the railway track and out to sea are obscured by the embankment – but the landscape is so rambunctious it feels like a very fair trade indeed to me.

It was only as I stood on the 17th tee, facing the steep dune ridge ahead that both my tee shot and my legs must climb, that this fact really become apparent. It's a routing that takes the player on a journey through different landscapes. It changes pace and direction often enough to keep all interest fixated on the here and now, rather than become distracted by what might be to come.

The carry up to the top is less challenging now than it might have been with hickory clubs, but still enough to focus the mind. In theory, it's a hole where you could cut off as much of the hill as your strength and pragmatism allow – and it therefore turns a functional climb into an enjoyable one.

The home hole completes the climb more gently in overall incline, but with as much movement over the fairway as anywhere else. It really is true linksland and the green at the end of it is as characterful as they come. Massive, it has tiers and contours requiring a deft closing touch to avoid a three putt that you might curse for your entire drive home.

I do hate using the term 'hidden gem'. Every gem is hidden from someone, and I imagine the members of most are happy keeping the courses they love and cherish to themselves. But, like Castletown, this is a course that receives less visitor play than might be expected. I have no doubt there will be people who will find it a little scruffy and the views of Sellafield too ugly to look beyond. But if you don't think these reasons are enough to put you off, I'd encourage anyone to pay the discounted late-afternoon green fee for what must be one of the best-value rounds in England. LFTR

022/225

St Bees

Owned by an ancient school that is still open today to serve its remote community, this nine-hole clifftop course is rapidly approaching its centenary

YOU can categorise the ownership of almost every course featured in these volumes as member- or proprietary-owned. Of these, it is the former which is most common. Privately owned courses are the clear minority across Britain in general.

If we did look at private owners, there might be some in the hands of a family, or perhaps a corporation specialising in owning and operating a handful of courses. Rarely will we find one owned by a school.

The school itself has been an independent school since its formation in 1583 by the then Archbishop of Canterbury Edmund Grindal. Grindal had been born in this isolated village, and the foundation of the school was one of his last acts, its formation finalised just days before his death.

For four centuries, the school educated a modest number of pupils across the 250 acres of windswept grounds on the Cumbrian coast. The school took it upon themselves to lay out a modest course just north of the village in the 1890s.

By the time a railway connected nearby Barrow-in-Furness to St Bees, it was decided the course should be relocated to a new location a short walk from the station. This 9-hole course was duly built and opened for play in 1929. While it had been funded by and was primarily for the school, locals were encouraged to be members of the club. This tradition continued until 2015 when poor finances closed the school. A groundswell from Old Beghians, former pupils of the school, raised the funds required to allow the school to reopen in 2018. Fortunately, the course survived and still serves this small community.

Rustic in style, this is played over as hilly a piece of terrain as you will find in a nine-hole seaside course. It was enough to make me wonder if returning Old Beghians might notice the walk in their legs more than they remembered from their school days.

The greens are small and basic but the views across to the Isle of Man up to St Bees Head must be beautiful on a clear evening. The highlight might be the downhill 3rd hole, driving blindly over the edge and scurrying anxiously after your ball in the hope of finding it on the fairway some 40 feet below. The 5th is another highlight. Again, driving blindly over a ridge – it is the view of St Bees Head and the cliff edge as you crest the ridge that provides the lasting memory. This is the one hole on the course with a few links contours on the approach to the green – which is sat handsomely into the base of a dune still far enough away to make you slightly concerned standing over your second shot.

St Bees probably isn't a course that even many devoted *Links from the Road* readers will find their way to, but it has played an important role in this little corner of the country – and clearly continues to do so. LFTR

The golf may be, in the main, relatively modest, at this nine-holer but the views out to sea surely make up for it

THE more courses I played throughout the tour, the more I found the courses on the edge of the links definition to be of interest. No one looks out across the rumpled fairways and dune ridges of Rye and wonders what style of golf it is. Likewise, no one would stand at Wentworth and confuse it with a links.

Maryport, however, is one that few of the people who enjoy engaging in this niche debate as much as I do seem to have visited. It is occasionally thrown round as a 'possible' – so I naturally had to visit and investigate for myself. It claims to have nine links holes and nine parkland holes. The small clubhouse is certainly sat close enough to the beach to give some optimism to the claim. Likewise, the 1st tee is as close to the water as you'll find – some rock armour and a mower's width of turf are the only separation from the lapping waves of the Solway Firth. Apparently, this opening run of holes has fallen victim to erosion in years past. Given that golf has been played here since 1905, it would not be the first course to have lost holes to the sea in the 20th century.

The result of the erosion is that the three remaining holes between the road and beach are rather cramped. Don't mistake that for short, though. Playing into a healthy breeze, with the road on the right and the beach on the left, the first two holes are both over 420 yards. Unfortunately, it's another

023/225

Maryport

A sliver of linksland hard against the waves of the Solway Firth offers reason enough to visit this blend of seaside and parkland

course that manages to stretch out the yardage with back tees added after the fact – indeed the 2nd tee is nearly 200 yards back down the fairway you have just walked.

The aspect is beautiful, and there are many courses featured over these volumes which don't enjoy such proximity to the water's edge. But by the time the nice 3rd hole has been played, we cross the road and lose sight of the sea.

The 4th plays through a corridor of thick gorse and the 5th is a nice par 3, but we then move up and over the hill and play back and forth through narrow avenues of trees.

The opening holes are so close to the water that it comes as no surprise to learn that coastal erosion has been an issue here

We do reappear down on the flatter land by the opening stretch when we reach the 16th hole. After a sense of claustrophobia among the woods, it made the reacquaintance with the long view of glistening water even more attractive.

Maryport is a nice course. For a green fee of £30 it's remarkable value. The greens rolled beautifully, and the scenery was quite beautiful. However it might be categorised – links, parkland, or a hybrid of the two – I'm sure the members and visitors who return will love it for what it is. LFTR

024/225

Silloth on Solway

Bringing back memories of childhood holidays, this Cumbrian links offers views across the firth to the promised land of Scotland and is bursting with character

I MUST put on record a sentimental attraction to the links at Silloth. There are reasons for this. One is its remoteness. It requires a concerted effort to get to Silloth. On this coast, it is the last English links before crossing the Scottish border and, like many of the courses featured in the latter half of this volume, the mountains and lakes of Cumbria create a physical boundary between motorway and sea.

The second reason is nostalgic. On a family holiday of my youth, it was one of the first links courses I played. Quite different from my native Hoylake, it helped spark an early love of the courses themselves. Years later, I returned soon after starting university. My parents had taken a cottage for a week in the north Lake District and suggested I take the train up to join them for a weekend. A reasonably attractive offer in itself, it became decisively so when my father said I should bring my clubs and we'd play Silloth again.

A rail journey with golf clubs melodiously clinking against the overhead luggage rack is always a nostalgic experience. A trip in the van excepted, of

The short 9th takes us alongside the Solway Firth

course, it is my preferred option of travelling to golf. I feel it connects the 21st and 19th century – Victorian tourists no doubt experienced the same feelings of anticipation and excitement at the prospect of a day on the links as we do. My parents met me at Carlisle station late on an autumnal evening and the following morning, Dad and I were first off at Silloth-on-Solway. Despite the years in between visits, I found I quickly remembered much of the course. It has so much quirk and individuality, it is hard not to.

The third reason I have a soft spot for the course is straightforward: it's seriously good.

So, while I have fond personal memories of taking the train to Silloth, the railway had a larger role in developing the area. It started with the Silloth Bay Project. Noting the existing Carlisle Bay port was silting up and proving difficult to navigate, a proper dock and rail link with the town was proposed in the 1850s. By the end of the decade, a daily steamer operated between the ports of Liverpool and Silloth – and the investment had proven a success. So much

Silloth on Solway
Hole 4, Par 4, 'The Mill'

McDonnell

Silloth's 4th is anything but run of The Mill. Described in more detail on Page 29 of this Volume, it encapsulates the quirk and charm of the entire course in miniature.

so, that when the dock suffered damage in the 1880s, it was a much larger and more significant structure that replaced it.

Silloth had ambitions of becoming a 'second Southport'. With easy travel links and an anecdotal reputation as having one of the best climates in the north of England, the North British Rail (NBR) company invested heavily in Silloth's infrastructure and marketing. Public baths were built and hotels and guest houses erected, all designed to strengthen Silloth's tourism credentials. If the objective was to encourage Scottish holidaymakers over the border to Silloth, then what could be better enticement than golf?

Fortunately, NBR's chairman was in full agreement. William Montagu Hay, the 10th Marquess of Tweedale, had been captain of North Berwick in 1890 and two years later it was professionals from the town tasked with laying out the first links at Silloth. Predominantly the work of Davie Grant, a famed North Berwick professional who had a fearsome golfing record in matches with his brother-in-law, Ben Sayers. He was assisted by the 1874 Open Champion, Mungo Park. Park, from the famous golfing family of Musselburgh, stayed on for a short while as Silloth's first professional. He repeated this combined role of architect and professional for a single year immediately afterwards at Portmarnock, in Dublin. The course was leased to the newly formed Carlisle and Silloth Golf Club for a peppercorn rent, but NBR still set the green fees and ensured visiting golfers had unfettered access to the links.

Through the years, the links has benefitted from the architectural input of some of the greats. Willie Park Jr. (Mungo's nephew, and the architect of Sunningdale Old and Maidstone, Long Island) reworked the course quite significantly in the years around the turn of the 20th century. Willie Fernie, the professional of Royal Troon, made further recommendations in 1912 and more significant proposals were laid out by the great Alister MacKenzie in 1915. Unfortunately, the ongoing hostilities prevented many of his ideas being adopted – but then the course that they left between them is not one that needs wholesale change anyway.

Before entering into any specifics, I think it's a course best described as polarising. Some dismiss it. Too many blind holes and quirky bounces. Scruffy in places and austere in setting – the town no longer the vibrant destination it was a century ago.

Others fall in deeply in love with it. I've heard well-travelled golfers rank it above the likes of Rye and Royal Cinque Ports. They swear it is only the isolated location and lack of a famous name that stop it being globally revered.

Naturally, after another decade or more since my last visit, I was eager to see where I might place it on this wide-ranging spectrum of opinion.

The opening hole does an excellent job in setting the tone for what follows. The drive is over rumpled ground, but the green is set down in a dell – obscured from the fairway. It won't be the last blind approach faced. The 2nd is to another tucked green, placed there over 130 years ago and left alone. It was often the case that in an era before irrigation systems, greens on free-draining sand would be placed at low points of the property. As well as creating a vexing challenge to approaches most often played along the ground, the grasses would have a better chance of surviving dry summer months by being where any water would more easily collect.

This was likely the case for the 3rd green at Silloth, but by the time MacKenzie visited, a better understanding of agronomy allowed this green to be moved on to the left – raised and set into a dune ridge. The new 3rd green led to a new 4th tee and this small change made a disproportionate improvement to the front nine.

Now, the 3rd is only a mid-length par 4 but it demands a pinpoint approach. The hole sweeps round to the left, the green slightly obscured from the tee by the sand hills that must be carried. An old road cuts diagonally across the fairway, and more thought must be given to a tee shot than might be expected on a bunkerless hole.

MacKenzie's 4th tee is another inspired change. As well as adding 100 yards, it was taking the tee to the left that I think makes it most interesting. The fairway pitches left to right and a tall dune obscures the direct line to the green. In short, everything – wind included – encourages play out to the clearer right side. But this hole isn't about the fairway, it's about the green. At 50-yards deep but only 18 wide – the drop off on either side is a good six feet. Too steep an angle to mow short, it requires a lobbed recovery shot – and I'm sure many a promising start to a medal round has been blown by chipping back and forth across this green. If ever there was a green to play to the front edge of, it might be this.

While the round to date has been somewhat introspective – focussing on intricate approach play, we move to the elevated 5th tee and marvel at the view across the eponymous Solway Firth. The estuaries of the Rivers Eden and Esk, this firth marks one of the natural boundaries between England and Scotland. It provides the backdrop to the most challenging drive faced thus far – the first par 5.

It's a hole that reminds me of some of the coastal holes at Royal St George's, with a raised tee playing obliquely to a crumpled fairway running parallel to the sea. It's the first time we notice how sparingly the bunkers have been used thus far. There are four cutting across the approach to the green in a diagonal echelon, when only three in total have been employed up to this point. While they might be the more obvious hazard here, it is more likely the contour and pitch of the fairway that will provide the greater challenge.

Next is a par 3 that gets harder every time you play it. Two bunkers set into the ridge partially obscure the green, itself pitched away from the tee, but it is the left one that defines the hole. It must be avoided to allow the ball to land and pitch forward. I'm convinced that with a trailing wind off the Firth and firm surfaces, anything landing on the green will run through. It must be one of the most visited bunkers.

Battery, the 7th hole, relies again on the contours and land rather than the bunkers to provide its challenge. A long drive helps, as the approach must make it to the top of the hill guarding the green – running all the way down the slope beyond and, with some luck, towards the hole. More likely, it will be repelled – and the recovery will be just beyond our wit.

By the end of the round, Silloth brings us back towards the industrial town with its distinctive Cumbrian brickwork

The 8th is a nice hole, but its greatest strength is in taking us to the 9th tee. Manx, named for the Isle of Man sometimes visible on the horizon, is special. There are plenty of parallels that can be drawn from other great one-shot holes. It is something of a mix between the 5th at Wallasey, if played from the high tee to the left, and the famous 8th at Royal Aberdeen.

The next three holes are all testing but allow the punch-drunk player to catch breath before reaching the extraordinary 13th. Of the thousands of holes I was lucky enough to play over my tour, I can confidently say this was unique. A former colleague, the walking encyclopaedia of golf course architecture, has a habit of making throwaway comments that stick long in my mind. He once quipped that the best

"Through the years, this links has benefitted from architectural input from some of the greats – including Willie Park Jr and Alister MacKenzie"

par 5s are fabulous drivable par 4s plus a drive. He could have been describing this hole.

Here, the drive of the hole called 'Hogs Back' is straightforward. No bunkers, no risky topography – just get into position, and don't mess it up. From this point, the fairway abruptly hits a steep wall of grass, and then continues a hill climb to a distant infinity green. Completely exposed to the elements, the green is the high point of the whole course – the fairway falling away precipitously on both sides.

With a sharp camber from left to right, even a short pitch after a sensible layup is terrifying. The only other hole I can think of that inspires such anxiety is the 4th at Rye.

From here, we face another par 5. Fortunately, this one is down the hill. Slightly longer than 13 but unquestionably easier. There are good holes on the closing stretch. The drive on 17 feels like it might be a distant relative of a Ganton 'Pandy' (covered in due course). The closing hole is strong – but perhaps on balance it is good for the blood pressure that the closing holes are, at least by comparison, relatively sedate.

Silloth really is an intriguing course. It is tight off the tee and generally with miniscule greens, but it feels playable. In terms of where the greens are placed, you'll struggle to find a more imaginative collection in England. For such bold fairways and green placement, the surfaces are pleasantly restrained. The challenge is in holding them, not in holing out.

For me, Silloth retains its special place in my heart. It's a fabulous course that far too many people pass by, but it's not perfect. I would go further and say it shouldn't strive to be.

I think a lot of what makes it so special is what prevents it from conquering the mainstream. The blind approaches, terrifying climbs, dodgy bounces and isolated location will always hold it back to some degree – but long may that continue. Appealing to the masses is a sure-fire way of losing one's individuality and soul – and Silloth is a place that has both in abundance. LFTR

What makes a links (continued)?

My initial musings in Volume 1 probably didn't satisfy you and it certainly didn't satisfy me. So let's see if I can improve on ,my definition here

AT the end of Volume 1, I mused at length over what makes a links course. The definitive answer to the question remained elusive. Clearly the standard definitions aren't up to scratch – so we moved beyond them to something a little more useful. Unfortunately, my analysis of the first dozen courses of the tour seemed to pose more questions than answers. In the end, the wholly unsatisfactory conclusion was "a course where a sufficient number of its holes are located on free draining, often sandy, terrain in close proximity to the sea". The exact number of holes, the proximity, the sandy ground itself – it is clear more work is required. At least the working definition remains sufficiently vague.

Volume 1 courses, including Southport Links and Leasowe, were stripped of the 'links' status given to them by Campbell & Peper in their 'definitive' book on the subject, 'True Links'. I also suggested The Warren, England's oldest municipal, should have been included in their list. If reflection on those courses was contentious, Volume 2 might prove more so. So let's start again with Campbell & Peper's book. The courses in this collection to have been featured in 'True Links' were Castletown, Fleetwood, Royal Lytham & St Annes, St Annes Old Links, Seascale and Silloth-on-Solway. No complaints here, all deserving of inclusion in my opinion.

Silloth is one of the most authentic links landscapes you can find – in many ways the purest links of this volume. Seascale is another that has more than enough links pedigree to warrant its place – as is St Annes Old Links. Fleetwood gets my vote for the time being but will be an interesting one to watch. It represents an interesting conundrum. For many courses on the tour, erosion and loss of land is a very real issue. Course 007, Formby, is one that has already suffered extensively. Royal Aberdeen and Montrose are examples that will be featured in later volumes. What these courses would give for a concrete sea defence. Wallasey benefits from one and, as of 2018, so does Fleetwood.

The long-term benefits are clear, but they must guard against subtle changes of character that can creep in almost unnoticed. A separation from the salt spray and sand blow can slowly change the agronomy of a site. The vegetation shifts, the fine grasses losing out to more agricultural variants. Land that once drained

easily into the beach might do so less readily. I am sure that Fleetwood will avoid these pitfalls, but the full effects will only be evident in the years to come.

Having warned against the pitfalls that can sometimes come with separation from the sea, Royal Lytham & St Annes is one with a few detractors. In 015, we discussed these nay-sayers who claim the trees down the 7th and houses that obscure any view of the sea mean it can't be a links. I would respectfully disagree.

Lytham manage their agronomy as well as anywhere, the incongruous trees that have grown up in the slightly more fertile part of the property not long for this world. As for the houses, they are hardly a fault of the course. The growth of Lytham & St Annes as a Victorian seaside resort led to significant development. An embankment was built in the late 1800s and land artificially reclaimed from the sea in the process. I think the land, the contour and a dozen other factors all mean Lytham's links status is not seriously in doubt.

Most interesting of this group is Castletown. Bluntly, Castletown isn't a pure links course – but a mix of styles. The extraordinary closing holes, playing along the rugged cliffs and crashing waves, are on the higher ground – a version of clifftop golf in my eyes. But, that said, plenty of the course is on pure links land. Especially the run of 6 through to 11, true and authentic links land. My vote is for keeping it in the links bracket – but I hope enough people visit this extraordinary spit of land for some to tell me I'm wrong. Whatever the designation, Castletown is worthy of your attention – I hope more people visit.

As we're in agreement with those they have included, have they missed any? Well, first and most obviously, Furness. How this was missed is a mystery to me – but they're not the only ones. Furness is just not on most people's radar. Despite being one of the oldest courses in England, with some brilliant holes, it doesn't seem to get talked about. Is it a links? For me, without doubt. There are more than enough true links holes here to deserve its place. Another I would like to propose is Dunnerholme. The stretch along the sandy Duddon Estuary is pure. Rumpled ground, fine grasses

"Vegetation across the site is important. Too many trees, too much gorse even, will fix nitrogen in the ground and, if left unchecked, change the character of a landscape beyond recognition"

and open vistas out to sea. Some will disagree, but I think this obscure 10-holer deserves links status. But of the Volume 2 courses, this would be my line in the proverbial sand. I don't think the nine holes draped over the cliffs at St Bees stake any claim. It is beautiful, but apart from a moment on the 5th, there is little to suggest it is more than a nice clifftop setting. Some will say Silecroft is a links, but I'd disagree. Maryport is one that does claim part links. Nine holes of parkland and nine of links for a hybrid links course, says the website. For me, there were three holes along the water that come close but fall short. The rest are unequivocal in their parkland nature. But is that a bad thing? A parkland that starts within touching distance of the water? It doesn't sound so bad to me.

Finally, we must consider Fairhaven. In 014, I described the 'inland links' course of sand and shaping that Braid created a century ago. That old course would split opinion – the perfect place to debate the near ineffable vagaries of this ancient form of the game. Unfortunately, it's not the course that exists today. The sandy, faux-dunescape that was created has grown over and the open landscape planted with trees and rhododendrons. What remains is an incredibly penal test, undoubtedly the 'championship test' the club claim it to be. But not a links. It does raise an interesting question for its

There can be no question that St Annes Old Links satisfies our criteria, even though the sea is rarely in the golfer's view

definition. While the agronomy has shifted as the vegetation has matured, there is still sand under the ground. There are holes at Fairhaven far closer to the beach than at Royal Lytham.

So, must we update our working definition after Volume 2? I think there are two clear variables that must feature. There are exceptions, as we know, but vegetation across the site must be important. Too many trees, too much gorse even, will fix nitrogen in the ground and, if left unchecked, change the character of a landscape beyond recognition.

"Fine grasses and firm golfing surfaces over rumpled, free draining ground that should – at one point in time – have a connection to the sea"

Clearly, we remain a work in progress. The better news is Volume 3 will take us to south-west Scotland. The home of golf has more links courses than anywhere else. There are examples with big dunes and tight, rippling contours. Massive maintenance budgets and miniscule. There is no shortage of contrast to come as we chart a course around this extraordinary golfing coastline. I hope you'll follow along. LFTR

My Favourite Places to...

Stay

From Blackpool Tower to Scafell Pike (England's highest peak at 3209 feet), the Fylde and Cumbrian coastlines have a lot to offer.

The Lake District is a beautiful place for a holiday for those family members less interested in the game of golf. Home to Beatrix Potter, John Ruskin, and The Lake Poets, notably William Wordsworth, Samuel Taylor Coleridge and Robert Southey - there's plenty for non-golfers to do, while you soak up the links courses along the coastline.

In Volume 1, it was straightforward to recommend a single location to enjoy every course featured. In Volume 2, it isn't. Geography and road networks complicate matters – and that's before we consider a trip to the Isle of Man for Castletown.

Therefore, I suggest it's a coastline better covered in two steps. Fortunately, they are two regions built for tourism – and there is no shortage of places to stay and enjoy yourself.

The first is the Fylde Coast. Royal Lytham & St Annes, Fairhaven, St Annes Old Links and Fleetwood can all be easily accessed from here. Blackpool might not be the destination it was in its heyday, but a 2023 survey still found it to be Britain's fifth-most-popular destination.

To the north, the Lake District National Park welcomes over 18 million visitors each year. There are 13 Michelin-starred restaurants to be found in the region that famously inspired the likes of William Wordsworth, Samuel Taylor Coleridge and Beatrix Potter. You must accept there will be some time on the roads while visiting the courses from Furness to Silloth, but driving through such picturesque environs will certainly make for a memorable trip.

Sleep

Dormy House, Royal Lytham and St Annes Golf Club

Almost as famous as the clubhouse itself, the dormy house of Royal Lytham and St Annes is iconic. Lytham is renowned for its hospitality and moving from spike bar to billiard room before finally retiring to a bedroom overlooking the 1st tee is as civilised as you can get.

Abbey House hotel, Barrow in Furness

This 4-star hotel is set in 14 acres of woodland on the outskirts of Barrow. Often overlooked as a location to stay, the hotel takes its name from the ruins of 900-year-old Furness Abbey, which is accessible through the grounds.

Storrs Hall, Bowness-on-Windermere

Originally built in 1790, this is the ultimate writers' retreat. Storrs Hall has played host to Beatrix Potter and Robert Southey. William Wordsworth even recited his most famous poem, "Daffodils", in the Drawing Room.

'Maid of Kent' Railway Carriage, Ravenglass

If a night in a van is too much of a stretch, how about a stay in an old railway carriage? On the west coast of the Lake District, you can stay in one of two sympathetically restored Pullman Camping Coaches. The Maid of Kent overlooks the Ravenglass and Eskdale railway line, home to five steam engines.

Rose Castle, Carlisle

If a railway carriage isn't grand enough, you can always hire the historic 800-year-old Rose Castle. Fifteen bedrooms and seven acres of grounds the perfect base for a unique golf trip.

Eat

Imli Indian restaurant, Lytham St Anne's

Mike Clayton says the first rule of tour is find a good Indian restaurant and go every night. This could fit the bill.

L'Enclume, Cartmel

Simon Rogan's three Michelin-starred restaurant L'Enclume has close ties to its home in the Lake District. Much of the produce used comes from the 12-acre farm on site. The restaurant sits within a 13th century blacksmith's workshop, the name 'L'Enclume' meaning 'anvil'.

The Drunken Duck, Ambleside

Famous throughout the Lake District and beyond, the Drunken Duck serves food as good as its ales – and that is saying something as the ales are pretty special.

Source at Gilpin Hotel & Lake House, Windermere

Set over several intimate dining rooms, head chef Ollie Bridgewater (formerly of Heston Blumenthal's The Fat Duck) crafts dishes that invariably focus on local ingredients at his own Michelin-starred restaurant.

Drink

The Swan, Grasmere

'Who does not know the famous Swan?'. These were the lines written in 1806 by Wordsworth, writing this inn into his poem 'The Waggoners' and, with it, history. Whether you are looking for a craft ale, a gin and tonic to sip on or a proper pot of English breakfast tea, soak up the history of this iconic pub.

The Lakes Distillery, Bassenthwaite Lake

Home of the 'World's Best Single Malt Whisky' 2022, The Lakes Distillery provide behind-the-scenes tours of their distillery with an expert guide. I'd recommend The Lakes Single Malt Whisky Experience if you would like to indulge your love of whisky.

The Ratty Arms, Ravenglass

Once familiar with the role the railway has played in developing golf in this corner of England, a pub set inside a former railway station might be more appealing. Watch the steam trains whistle by as you enjoy a drink.